Lerma Novales Sarmiento was married and born originally in the Philippines. She is the third child among eight siblings. She left the country at a very young age to work as a domestic helper in another country in order to financially support her family.

Dear Johan, Jobel, Jakob & JJ,

Walking in the Spirit will lead to have a peaceful and joyful life. The presence of the Holy Spirit will always be on your side. Let the Holy Spirit be the center of our lives and the fruits of the Holy Spirit will bless your house and family to have a fulfilled life.

Love,
Lerma Novales Sarmiento
Sarmiento
(Ate Emma)

I dedicate this book to all the souls that are lost and broken-hearted and pray that they may find true happiness and realise that they are not living alone. And may they receive the Holy Spirit into their life.

Lerma Novales Sarmiento

LIFE IN THREE PARTS

AUSTIN MACAULEY PUBLISHERS™

LONDON • CAMBRIDGE • NEW YORK • SHARJAH

A CIP catalogue record for this title is available from the British Library.

ISBN 9781528981668 (Paperback)
ISBN 9781528981675 (ePub e-book)

www.austinmacauley.com

First Published (2021)
Austin Macauley Publishers Ltd
25 Canada Square
Canary Wharf
London
E14 5LQ

I thank God, Jesus and the Holy Spirit for the gift of wisdom. Without the presence of their spirit into my life, I couldn't have created this book.

Table of Contents

Introduction

Corinthians 6: 119-20

Do you not know that your bodies are temples of the Holy Spirit, who is in you, whom you have received by God? You are not your own; you were bought at a price. Therefore, honour God with your bodies.

Inside of us, there is an inner voice that wants us to know about His presence in our lives and journey with Him in everyday of our lives and that is the Holy Spirit. God said, *When you received the gift of my son, Jesus, you received me.*

Jesus was sent by our Almighty Father to be the light of this world. And anyone who believes in Him should not perish, but have the grace of the inheritance of eternal life. Jesus was born of Mary by the grace of the Holy Spirit and was sent by our Almighty Father to bring back the love and the peace in this world. Jesus is the exact representation of God that He is with us and we belong to Him. The kingdom of heaven is revealed to Jesus, and through and by Jesus only, for he is the firstborn child of the Holy Spirit that is born in the Spirit. God's love must be revealed, also, to us through the grace and truth of the words of Jesus. It is said, *Seek first the kingdom of heaven and this will be added unto you.*

Adversity in life is a test of our faith, which must go through the fire of pain and suffering. It is said, *God is very close to the broken-hearted.* And that is the moment we should call upon God to help us to be out of wrath in our life. But we humans always seek help in others rather than God.

God is the creator of heaven and earth and He knows the heart of all His children. God said that all His people are lost because of a lack of knowledge. Humans always lean on their

11

own understanding that brings them more pain and suffering. God said, "My thought is not your thought," therefore, we should submit our hearts through prayers by having a conversation with God. Our soul must be connected to the supernatural power of the Holy Spirit. And we should let the Holy Spirit lead our lives to live on this planet. Jesus said that our bodies are the temples of the Holy Spirit and we commit unforgivable sins when we slander the Holy Spirit. Jesus was called to be the Messiah and chosen child of God that would baptise people by the grace of the Holy Spirit. Jesus said that He and the Father are one because the truth is that the real Father of Jesus was the Holy Spirit, and Joseph was only his former father. Joseph was from the clan of David, which in turn was the clan of Abraham. Jesus did not come from the clan of Abraham but He was born in the presence of the Almighty Father. This is the reason why Jesus did not recognise his earthly parents as his real parents. For Jesus, his real parent is the Almighty Father which is invisible to the eyes but known in the heart, for God looks upon the heart and his lamb as well. Heaven is revealed through the nature of Spirit and not by the flesh. Jesus said that He will leave us the Holy Spirit as our helper. And this is our gift from him but God said, "When you receive the gift of my son Jesus you received me."

In the teaching of Jesus, he did not say that his Father is the Holy Spirit. But the story of how Jesus was born into this world is completely different. He was born from the power of the Holy Spirit. Jesus said that He and the Father are one because they are both living at the same nature of the Holy Spirit. Journeying with the Holy Spirit makes us feel secured. The gift of the Holy Spirit will bring us fulfilment. God is love, and we are formed also to be called love. For we are children of God like Jesus. Revolution of the Spirit is putting our soul to cleansing out from death. The wage of sins is death through repentance and accepting Jesus, and treating our bodies as the temples of the Holy Spirit in our heart are seeing heaven here on earth. Our soul is sound and safe in the presence of the Holy Trinity (The Father, the Son and the Holy Spirit). Grace in heaven is revealed to us here on earth.

Many are called to believe in Jesus but only a few are chosen. Jesus is the way, the life and the truth. No one can come to the Father without accepting Jesus' teaching, as the living water that will nourish our souls to set our hearts to get as spiritually matured. Look upon the one we cannot see for that is eternal; the things we can see of our sight are only temporary.

Part-One
Living Your Life in a Godly Way

Theology

The field of study and analysis that treats God and of God's attributes, and their relations to the universe, the study of divine things of religious truth and of divinity.

Wisdom

The quality or state of being wise; knowledge of what is true or right coupled with just judgment as to action; sagacity, discernment, or insight.

Matthew 6:33

But seek first the kingdom of God and His righteousness, and all these things will be added to you.

2 Corinthians 4:18

So we fix our eyes not on what is seen but on what is unseen since what is seen is temporary, but what is unseen is eternal.

God is love and His love comes eternally with unlimited supply. And you will find this everywhere.

Awareness leads our thinking to great wisdom, by knowledge and understanding to differentiate such things with power and majesty. We must jump to the unknown place and dig it out. It is like finding gold and diamond, we need to mine it out. But without focus, time and effort you would not be able to find it. In life, these three aspects are the tools and strategies of setting your mind to the unknown.

Remember that a reward does not come easily to someone who easily wants to give up. The power is in our thoughts, in how you project your mind towards creating this energy within you. And this energy will create and produce something from your actions which is called experience.

Remember that we are not just human beings living in flesh but are all created by the same God.

Focus on the words of God and He will guide you. See, we are only travellers in this world. Our life here on Earth is only a journey to find out our way back home. See, the reality is that our lives here on Earth has a beginning and an end. Each one of us has the purpose to find out where we belong.

Life is a journey with good days and bad days. This is the way that God will train and give us greater lessons about life.

Through our experiences, we will be strained, battered in troubles until we get to the point where we realise that every situation that we have encountered in life, has a reason behind it. And when we find and seek out that reason we are able to understand that God did not put us to the test to harm us but that He wants us all to prosper ourselves with the help of His unconditional love, mercy and compassion.

Life is like an oracle. You will put your heart to find out the beauty of it, in knowing where it comes from and knowing who owns it. Life has a symbol like a labyrinth but has to be put to test. Of course, if you see yourself in it, you should look at the passage that will lead you to the very end.

How This Book Can Be used

I certainly open up my heart and mind to have a conversation with anyone. Knowing and finding ourselves who we really are, within ourselves.

From science, we know that everything that we see in this world comes from evolution. But beyond that, I found out that there is something far more executing than that. The question in my mind was *where the evolutions come from?*

In our world where we live, some people do not believe in God. In the Bible, it is written that Thomas was one of the disciples of Jesus who was the true Son and servant of the Lord. But then after the crucifixion, when Jesus was being resurrected, Thomas did not believe.

In the Gospel of John 20:24-28, it is written, *Thomas, the Twin, one of the Twelve, was not with them when Jesus came. The other disciples told him, "We have seen the Lord." But he replied, "Until I have seen in his hands the print of the nails, and put my finger in the mark of the nails and my hand in his side I will not believe."*

Eight days later, the disciples were inside again and Thomas was with them. Despite the locked doors Jesus came and stood in their midst and said, "Peace be with you!"

Then He said to Thomas, "Put your finger here, and see my hands; stretch out your hand, and put it into my side. Don't be an unbeliever! Believe."

Thomas then said, "You are my Lord and my God." Jesus replied, "You believe because you see me, don't you? Happy are those who have not seen, but believe."

Jesus was inviting us all to put our heart in service for the Lord. Proclaiming the Gospel, nowadays, to others is not easy, for you will be persecuted and hated by others.

In the Gospel of John 15:18-19 said,

If the world hates you, remember that the world hated me before you. This would not be so if you belong to the world, because the world loved its own. But you are not of the world, since I have chosen you from the world; because of this, the world hates you.

Knowing about the life of Jesus is like a stream that will nourish our life to live a Godly life. We will pass our days with faith, hope and love. It is time for us to question, *Do we act like obeying God like Jesus did? Or are we still like Adam and Eve who were our first earthly parents, and who disobeyed God?*

How the Book Is Set-Up

There will be some home-bound buddies that I would recommend to understand the true nature about life.

What is the true value of life?

What was the reason that Jesus chose to suffer, to be nailed and died on to the cross?

As all of us can see, all human beings have different colours, shapes and sizes, and cultures, traditions and beliefs. That blinds our understanding that we are all equally created by God.

We have forgotten that we came from the very essence of the Spirit of the Lord that is why we live and move our being. Every soul matters to God, and that is the reason that He sent Jesus to this world so that through him the love of the Lord will be revealed to us and from then we would be able to love God and lean on God and not on our own understanding. We all have been given the life to live to be in this world temporarily so that the wonders of God will be realised and known also to us to understand that nothing is impossible to God.

The Story of First Creation

In the beginning when God began to create the heaven and earth, the earth had no form and was void; darkness was over the deep and the Spirit of God hovered over the waters. In six days God created the world as a paradise to live. He put humans in charge to govern everything. God created humans to His likeness and image, this is the reason why humans have more knowledge and wisdom than the animals. This is the reason why we have the;

Farmers Pilot

Architects Drivers

Doctors Safeguards

Scientist Chef

Teacher Marines

Policemen and many more

These people have the knowledge to share their gifts and talent with others and the community. Their purpose is to unite the community, to build a nation and help in making the world a better place. Every person is beautiful to God because they all have the capability to co-create and have the purpose to share the love to look after each other.

Wisdom Is from God

Jeremiah 118:4

But the pot he was shaping from the clay was marred in his hands; so the potter formed it into another pot, shaping it as seemed best to him.

In the history of the world, in scientific research, dinosaurs were found to be the first living creation that lived in the planet. They have found some fossils and added to the history of the world. This could be probably true and their extinction was brought about by an asteroid shower. It is highly probable that dinosaurs were eliminated from this world because they didn't have the knowledge to co-create like us, human beings. Dinosaurs must be considered only as a pet for God. But the figure of these animals was merely common in some animals that we may see in this world. And in this world where we are living, we are divided in seven continents. It has not been proven, however, that dinosaurs lived in all these continents. Scientists have found out only some specific places where these animals existed.

Every creation we see with our eyes is wonderfully made by the love of God. Our world should be a place and paradise for us to live. We all have come from the very omnificent presence of the Spirit of God. Every creation is perfectly made from the words of God and has their own purpose and meaning in this entire world.

Because of the sins we inherited from our first earthly parents, Adam and Eve, the world was been transformed into a battlefield between good and evil. Humans have been transformed into a greater predator in this world and have lost the sense to differentiate between light and dark.

Hatred covered each humans' heart with pain and suffering and is doomed in this world. People are being contaminated by the evil desire towards to one another. They have the desire to being competitive to each and every one. They are fighting for the riches of the world and want to take away others' possessions to be the best and greater than anyone else, even God. Most people have turned away their hearts from God and have chosen their own ways to live. They have just lost their self-control not knowing who and where they come from. It is so sad that majority of all the people in this world have hearts turned rebelliously against God, our lovingly creator and Father of all.

Genesis 2:115-17

Yahweh took man and placed him in the Garden of Eden to till it and take care of it. Then Yahweh God gave an order to man saying, "You may eat of every tree in the garden, but of the tree of the Knowledge of Good and Evil, you will not eat, for on the day you eat of it, you will die."

Adam and Eve were living in a paradise which was innocent and had no sins. God forbid Adam not to eat, even touch, the fruit of this tree of Knowledge of Good and Evil because Satan had an interest to deceive God's precious child and formed it to a rebellious child of God. But Eve was deceived by Satan and she invited Adam to eat the forbidden fruit. Adam and Eve disobeyed God. They were deceived by Satan. They ate the fruit because Satan said, "You will be like God if you come to know the difference between good and evil." God found out that Adam and Eve did not listen to Him, and that is why they became sinners. And from that time they were contaminated by the mark of the beast, which is why they lost their light and the inheritance of eternal life.

Romans 6:23

The wage of sins is death, but the gift of God is eternal life with Christ Jesus, our Lord.

Yahweh ordered Adam and Eve not to eat the fruit of knowledge of good and evil because God knew that the Paradise He created for his children would become like a battle field between good and evil. People would lose their titles as a children of God, for the light and life that was given to them would come to diminish because of the darkness of sins. Satan manipulated and deceived people. The world that had been paradise for the child of God was transformed into a zone for the Zombies. Yes, even we exist in this world, our soul is in condemnation of darkness of sins. No one can ever escape unless we accept Jesus in our hearts, minds and souls to be the light for our life. Who will baptise us by the Holy Spirit and be born again as a new creation of God? Through repentance our sins will be forgiven, and then the body, which is the temple of God, will be illuminated by the grace and love of God and the Holy Spirit. Satan has no power anymore over us to deceive because we choose to love and forgive ourselves, which will give merit to our souls. The Holy Trinity, which is God the Father, The Son and the Holy Spirit will lead and guide us to the way that we should go.

Ecclesiastes 112:7

And the dust returns to the ground it came from, and the Spirit returns to God who gave it.

Human has been given only a limited time to live because we are only travellers in this world. No one is the best or superior to anyone else. The time comes that God will come to us like a theft without any warning. He will come back to us at unexpected times and day to take away the breath that He had bestowed upon us. Our souls are part of a Spirit who gives life to our bodies that is why we live and move our beings, this does not belong to us, for this belongs to God. No one man has the power to create a soul in this world. This is the reason why Jesus rejected the offer of Satan to have the riches of this world. He said to Satan, "Do not put to the test your God." Because the Kingdom of God is formed by Spirit and not by flesh because this was a belonging to the earth. This is the reason why Jesus said that His kingdom is not here on earth but in heaven.

Adam and Eve put themselves to follow Satan, this is the reason why they were cast out from the Garden of Eden. The world has been full of violence, hatred, no life at all because the wages of the works of sins is death for each soul who we did not put the heart in seeking God and asking for his forgiveness. Repentance can be done only until the Spirit of the Lord is not departing yet to our body. But once this is gone this will be too late. Because our body will be put to the grave or cremation but our soul will come to face for our judgment according to our deeds.

God had sent Jesus to the world to be the light in this world so that through Him we have the access to gain to have the life again and inherit the eternal life.

From the time that Adam and Eve ate the fruit Satan entered to put one soul and the other in the condemnation of darkness of sins.

God forbid Adam and Eve not to eat the fruit of knowledge between good and evil because in He knew Satan will condemn the soul of all humankind to pain, crying and suffering. Satan will rule the world by the darkness of sins. Humankind will be blind of not knowing the truth of value, and the mystery of life does come from the infinite source of Spirit and not by the flesh alone. Most people will adore to make pleases their flesh which comes from dust rather than the Spirit which is the source of their life that is why they live and move their being.

2 Corinthians 14

And no wonder, for Satan himself masquerades as an angel of light.

Hosea 4:6

My people are destroyed for lack of knowledge; because you have rejected knowledge, I reject you from being a priest to me. And since you have forgotten the law of your God, I also will forget your children.

Satan is a great pretender and deceiver. He raised himself as God and allowed people to believe in him. He is corrupt because he confuses the minds of people. He won't give justice to people, he adores and loves people to live in lies and unrighteousness.

Adam had intercourse with Eve, his wife. She became pregnant and gave birth to a child. She named him Cain, then later on she gave birth to Abel. Because Adam and Eve disobeyed God, the world will be governed by the law of Satan for the next generations. Satan pretended to be God. He confused the mind of a person that is why Cain killed his brother, Abel. Satan contaminated one heart by marking pride in the hearts of people, this is the reason that people are acting like beasts and enemies to others, who are our brothers in the same image of God.

Proverbs 8:13

To fear the Lord is to hate evil; I hate pride and arrogance, evil behaviour and perverse speech.

Proverbs 11:2

When pride comes, then comes disgrace, but with humility comes wisdom.

Satan pretended himself to be a good friend and played tactics with Adam and Eve, which is the reason why they were deceived. The fruit of the tree that was eaten by Adam and Eve is poisoned by pride. This is the reason why the world is full of hatred and violence. Pride is the mark of the beast which has been marked in every human heart. Pride is satanic and it brings conflicts in the life of everyone's soul.

Satan started to rule the world and made himself known as God but not Father for all because he is not loving, caring and does not give fair treatment to all. He was playing favourites to deceive one heart and another to walking their life rebelliously to God. He put jealousy and anger in the minds and hearts of people, which is why their souls are in darkness of hell of sins. This is the reason that the first child of Adam and Eve killed his brother. Satan took the place to stand as the Father of Abel but not for Cain even though they both came from Adam and Eve. For Cain and Abel Yahweh, God is their real Father and their life belongs to God but this God which was encountered by Cain was not the real loving, caring and merciful God but it was Satan. From the time this God reject the gift of offerings of Cain, the sins have been multiplying.

As we can see if this is a truly loving God. He will be merciful and compassionate to his child. He will not play favourites to love one and hate the other. He will not put Cain's mind and heart to turn evil to his brother. Then this God is wondering and asking innocently to Cain, "Why are you angry and downcast? What kind of God is this?" He doesn't know and understand why Cain did that. Does it mean this God has no common sense to understand that Cain turns evil to kill his brother because of rejecting the gift that is offered to this deceiving god, he is not being fair, loving and merciful to Abel and Cain? Satan is a great pretender and deceiver. After Cain killed his brother, Satan cursed Cain by saying, "You will be a fugitive wandering on earth."

Cain did not understand that Satan was using God's name just to deceive him.

Genesis 4:13-14

Cain said to Yahweh, "My punishment is greater than I can bear. See, today you drive me from this land. I must hide from you and be a wanderer and fugitive on earth and it will so happen that whoever meets me will kill me." Yahweh said to him, "Well then, whoever kills Cain will suffer vengeance seven times."

See how evil this work is! This Yahweh will rather like to multiply the sins than to give forgiveness, mercy and compassion to Cain. If I stand as Cain I will offer to this Yahweh to take my breath away so that the sins stopped and not be multiplied. And this deceiving God is the one who must take the vengeance to suffer seven times. Therefore, Satan will never have the access to ruin one heart and one soul.

Differences That Need to Be Recognised

From the beginning, God forbid Adam and Eve not to eat the fruit of knowledge. But Adam and Eve did not listen and disobeyed God that is the reason why they have been deceived by Satan. The mind of people was formed to have the knowledge and given the idea to strain the thoughts between good and evil but most people in the world does not have self-control to think which one they will have to pursue which will benefit through a fulfilling life.

Looking back at the time of history of the life of Noah. Most people did not listen to Noah because he was a drunkard. Most people questioned Noah's identity, this is the reason why they won't listen to Noah. What happened to the people who were drowned and died in the flood. This doesn't mean that these people who did not rescue themselves from the flood it means they were living in hell for it just been told that we were be judge according to our deeds (Romans 2:6) and in 2 Corinthians 5:10 it is said that, "For we must all appear before judgement seat of Christ, so that each of us may receive what is due us for the things done while in the body, whether good or bad."

Perhaps, most people in that time did not listen to Noah because they thought Noah was a drunkard and it might possibly be that the thoughts of Noah were lost because of the alcohol that he had drank. As I continued reading the story of Noah, I found that this God is not perfect, He made mistakes and accept to himself that he will not be ruined again the world that is why he said to Noah, (Genesis 9: 14-17) "When I bring clouds over the earth and the rainbow appears in the clouds I will remember the covenant between me and you and every kind of living creature, so that never again will floodwaters destroy all flesh. When the rainbow is in the clouds, I will see it and remember the everlasting covenant between God and every living creature of every kind that exists on the earth."

God said to Noah, "This is the sign of the covenant. I have been made between me and all that has life on the earth."

Matthew 24:35

Heaven and earth will pass away, but my words will not pass away.

Our soul belongs to the kingdom of God and our body belongs to the earth. This will prove that once a person who was created by God departs this world this person has no more purpose to live at all and this will pass away but the evolutions of life will still continue to evolve in generations to generations therefore this creation will not pass away.

List of Nations

There are only the descendants of Noah who had been foretold about their family who is been save by the flood. But in the world where we are living in now, we are divided into seven continents which are:

North America
South America
Antarctica
Europe
Asia
Africa
Australia

Through this I questioned in my mind from that time.

Did Noah research and travel to these other continents?

Did he explore the world really? It seems not, and if he did why he is so sure to himself that their family is the chosen one which to be the God's favourite?

How about the other people from another nation? Haven't been they created from the same image of God?

I found that who made the story about the history of the life of Noah and his descendants until to the life of Moses is a myth made from fiction to confuse the mind of people because the truth about the true personality of one Almighty God was not clear to them.

The flood story tells how Noah and his three sons Shem, Ham and Japheth, together with their wives were saved from the deluge to repopulate the earth. In the story it is said that Noah is a drunkard. But I am wondering why he gets mad at his son Ham when he sees him naked because he was passed out from his drink? Ham tells his brothers and his brothers put robes over their shoulders and walk backwards into the tent, so that they won't actually see their father naked, and they cover him with the robe. But when Noah wakes up and find out what Ham did, and he curses Ham to be the slave of his brothers.

It seems Noah got furious with Ham because he was ashamed of himself and the only way to get rid of his anger and satisfy himself is to curse Ham. Where is the justice in there? How cruel is that? He cursed Ham his son because he found him naked. In this real world if that would come to happen. I would rather to teach a lesson and let him realise what he has done was absolutely embarrassing. So don't ever try to put that guilt to anyone to make as guilty of something because of your insanity of losing of out of control. Use your mind properly so that next time you know what will be the cause of your works for being drunk. It is really true most children of God are lost because of the lack of knowledge. They cannot depend on people who are selfish and have the hearts of the beast. Who made the story of Noah was really have the heart of the beast and his works must only pleasing evilness than holiness? Noah curses Ham because that anger, bitterness and resentment are easy to multiply. Therefore, family must go hand in hand to love one another. Forgiveness has no place in everyone's heart because the pride is in-charge to rule one soul and the other to be ruined by pain, crying and suffering.

Jesus is the true Messiah and the light of the world. Through him the divine personality of God has been revealed. God is loving, patient, merciful and full of compassion towards all His people and His children. He knows deep in His heart that all His children make mistakes because of lack of knowledge. He is not distant or angry but he has the complete expressions of love. He is patient to let his children learn to gain some lessons from their experiences and hope to do so to motivate their selves to change their hearts so that they will walk their heart into repentance and sin no more so that we will gather as all again to love and be loved by one another.

The Tower of Babel

Genesis 11:1-9 "The whole world had one language and a common speech." As people moved from east, they found a plain in the country of Shinar where they settled. They said to one another, "Come, let us make bricks and bake them in fire." They used brick for stone and bitumen for mortar. They said also, "Come, let us build ourselves a city and a tower with its top reaching heaven; so that we may become a great people and not be scattered over the face of the earth." Yahweh came down to see the city and the tower that the sons of man were building, and Yahweh said, "They are one, people and they had one language. If they carry this through, nothing they decide to do from now on will be impossible. Come, let us go down and confuse their language so that they will no longer understand each other." So Yahweh scattered them over all the earth and they stopped building the city. That is why it was called Babel because there, Yahweh confused the language of the whole earth and from there Yahweh scattered them over the whole face of the earth.

In the world where we live now, there are so many countries and different languages but there is still one language and common speech that will be given to us all to recognise the value to put things together in common and has the senses to understand each meaning. English is this language and this is recognised in the whole continents of the world. Some people, though, still believe in that ancient time that reaching heaven is like building a tower and if they can do that they will become known as a great people and not be scattered over the face of this earth. But as we can see now, airplanes and jets are reaching so high to fly in the sky and it is so much higher than building a tower of Babel. But even if you go to the sky and you try to reach places like the planet Mars heaven cannot be proven to find these ways. It is said that Yahweh confused the language of the whole earth and scattered these people over the whole face of the earth. I found in my heart that this God is really confusing and not loving, merciful and full of compassion towards people. Because this God is not the same God as Jesus is preaching.

(John 8:21) Once more Jesus said unto them, "I am going away, and you will look for me, and you will die in your sin. Where I go, you cannot come."

Jesus said in these ways because heaven is not something that you can see with your eyes. It is something understood by wisdom that comes from the inner part of the heart. Heaven is something mysterious that you will not be able to gain if you do not repent for your sins and be baptised by the Holy Spirit. This is the reason why Jesus said that He will go away and will look for him but we were not able to go where He goes because Jesus knows that the wages of sins are death, through sins each soul will be killed and has ended into the darkness of hell of pain and suffering. After our days to live have ended in this world, it is our soul who will face the time of judgement and not our flesh for it is said that our flesh is from our body and our body is from dust and this will return to dust. Through repentance and changing our heart to love the Spirit who is living within us by turning away from sins and believing in Jesus, we can journey with Jesus as long as his teachings are fully alive in our minds, heart and soul. This is the only way we will find the elusive peace and security in life. Even Jesus does not exist anymore in this world. If you put in your heart all his teachings he will not depart from you until your last breath for he will be your light, and the gift that you have received from him will be your guide for the rest of your life. So, we can see that every person has limited time to journey in this world.

But the question is, will every soul be saved without repenting from sins once these people were departed from this world?

Jesus reminds people to repent and sin no more and if we did not listen to him and stop sinning again and again something even worse might happen to us. (Matthew 7:21-23) Jesus says, "Not everyone who says to me, 'Lord, Lord', will enter the kingdom of heaven, but he who does the will of my Father who is in heaven will enter. Many will say to me on that day, 'Lord, Lord, did we not prophesy in your name, and your name cast out demons, and in your name perform many miracles?' And then I will declare to them, 'I never knew you; depart from me, you who practice lawlessness.'"

Matthew 24:4-5

Jesus answered, "Be on your guard and let no one mislead you. Many will come, claiming my title and saying: 'I am the Messiah', and they will mislead many people."

People who acted as if they were saviours and holy are usually attending church or religious functions, singing in the church choir, lifting their hands at church, and being very excited about Jesus in their functional groups. These people are more focused on the title of their religions or Christian communities and not on the teachings of Jesus. They don't show respect to the Holy Spirit because they were formed to be divided by their title. Some people are idolising their ministers, and they have put their hearts to fight if someone insults their idol. Religions in this world are only propaganda for making titles and money. Jesus commands us all to love one another but many false priests and prophets were not followers of Jesus Christ because they will rather condemn one soul and another for the sake of the name of their religions. They were so attached and loving to the title of their religions and ministers and not to the teachings of Jesus. Even though they will preach about Jesus but their heart is closed and their minds are not open to the truth. They don't understand that the words and teachings of Jesus are the body and blood of Jesus that will give wisdom and knowledge to understand the mystery of life who put himself as a sacred living sacrifice that will help to every soul to live in the presence of the Lord until we depart in this world.

Mark 4:12

Jesus says, "They see what I do, but they don't perceive its meaning. They hear my words, but they don't understand. So they will not turn from their sins and be forgiven."

The point is, even you can appear to be the holiest person on earth but if you will not be baptised by the Holy Spirit through Jesus Christ, you still missed Heaven and spend your life in eternal hell. You can appear to have your act together with the Lord in the presence of others, but God knows the true condition of each people's mind and heart.

Fruits of the Descendants of Noah

Adultery, murderer, corrupt, jealousy, etc. are formed with this family. And if God is with them why does this God allow this to make it to happen if they were the chosen people in the whole wide world? Does it mean this is not the real God?

The Call of Abram

(Genesis 12:1-3) Yahweh said to Abram, "Leave your country, your family and your father's house, for the land I will show you. I will make you a great nation. I will bless you make your name great, and you will be a blessing. I will bless those who bless you, and whoever curses you, will curse and in you all the people on the earth will be blessed."

Later on I will write what Abram has done and this makes us question why this God is so sure to say that through Abram all the people on the earth will be blessed?

So, Abram went as Yahweh had told him. Abram was seventy-five years old when he left Haran. Abram took Sarai, his wife, his nephew Lot, all the possessions they had accumulated and the people they had acquired in Haran. They set out for the land of Canaan. They arrived at Canaan. Abram travelled through the country as far as Shechem, to the oak of Moreh. At that time the Canaanites were in the land. Yahweh appeared to Abram and said, "To your descendants, I will give this land." There he built an altar to Yahweh who had appeared to him.

Yahweh appeared to Abram.

(John 4:24) *Jesus said that God is a Spirit and his worshippers must worship in the Spirit and truth.*

(John 5:37) Jesus said, "Thus he who bears witness to me is the Father who sent me. You have never heard his voice and never seen his likeness; therefore, as long as you do not believe his messenger, his word is not in you."

(Corinthians 3:16) *Don't you know that your selves are God's temple and that God's Spirit dwells in your midst?*

So I wondered how it is that Yahweh has appeared to Abram and Abram built an altar for Yahweh.

Honestly, no one can ever hear the voice or see the appearance of God for He is a Spirit and He dwells in our selves. No one can ever understand the personality of God unless these people receive the gift of the Holy Spirit through Jesus Christ. God said, "If you seek me with all your heart, you will find me and I will reveal myself to you." From then we were able to understand what is in the mind and the desire of the heart of Jesus. God is a Spirit and our soul is the masterpiece of God's Spirit which has made us God's offspring, through that we live and move our beings. God also said, "When you received the gift of my son Jesus you received me." Our heart will be the altar for the Lord and our body should be the temple of God, our lips should be used as the church that will proclaim the Gospel of the light, the way and the truth by the grace and the help of the Holy Spirit.

Genesis 12:10-13

There was a famine in the land and Abram went to Egypt to stay there for some time, for the famine was severe in the land. Just as he was about to enter Egypt he said to Sarai, his wife, "Now I know you are a beautiful woman. When the Egyptians see you they will say; that is his wife! They will then kill me, but they will let you live. Say that you are my sister, so they treat me well on account of you and my life will be spared because of you."

Matthew 10:28

Do not be afraid of those who kill the body but cannot kill the soul. Rather, be afraid of the one who can destroy both soul and body in hell.

Abram had a corrupt mind. He was afraid to lose his life that is why, he told Sarai, his wife to not tell the truth so that his life will be spared. Abram was not being honest and truthful about himself and the others. Abram was a liar and a great pretender.

(Matthew 16:25) *For whoever wants to save their life will lose it, but whoever loses their life for me will find it.*

Does Abram praise the same God who had sent Jesus into this world? Abram does not have wisdom like Jesus, for he did not understand that all people have only limited time to live. We have only been given a certain amount of days to travel in this world. Abram did not understand that the life of a man depends on the Spirit who is living amongst us and not through the flesh itself.

(Genesis 3:19) *By the sweat of your brow, you will eat your food until you return to the ground, since from it you were taken; for dust you are and to dust you will return.*

Ecclesiastes 12:7

And the dust returns to the ground it came from, and the Spirit returns to God who gave it.

This will prove that no man on this earth has the power to live eternally in this world. Even the prophets are gone, for it is our soul that gives life and is the source of strength to our body and that has belonged to God who guides our bodies.

Genesis 12:14-20

When Abram arrived in Egypt, the Egyptians saw that the woman was very beautiful. Pharaoh's officials saw her and praised her to Pharaoh. The woman was taken to the

Pharaoh's house and because of her he dealt well with Abram; he received sheep, cattle, donkeys, menservants, maidservants, she-asses and camels. But Yahweh inflicted severe plagues on Pharaoh and his household because of Sarai. So Pharaoh summoned Abram and said, "What have you done to me? Why did you say; she's my sister so that 1 took her for my wife. Now here is your wife! Take her and go!" And Pharaoh gave orders to his men regarding Abram, and they sent him on his way, with his wife and all that was his.

Both Abram and Sarai had the corrupt minds and they deceived the Pharaoh for not telling the truth. This is the reason why Pharaoh caught into severe plagues and his household because of Sarai. Pharaoh took Sarai as to be his wife without having the knowledge about the truth.

Is the god of Abram kind, loving and merciful for what Abram and Sarai had done to Pharaoh and his household? Abram's god is only a deceiver that will turn evilness to other houses like as Pharaoh.

Why this god allowed Abram and Sarai to sin not telling the truth? This god allowed Sarai to commit adultery with the Pharaoh and blessed Abram to received sheep, cattle, donkeys, menservants, maidservants, she-asses and camels.

Doesn't this God know that adultery is a great sin which will put one soul into darkness, death and into the fires of hell? It seems that this one is not the same God that Jesus was talking to.

Genesis 13:1-4

Abram went from Egypt to the Negeb, he and his wife with all he had and lot with him. Now Abram was very rich in flocks, silver and gold. As he journeyed on, he went from the Negeb as far as Bethel to the place where he first pitched his tent between Bethel and Ai at the spot where he had formerly maid an altar and called on the name of Yahweh.

Because of the lie that Abram and Sarai had told the Pharaoh, they got all these riches. He used to give blessings to Abram by allowing Sarai by committing adultery.

What would you think of it?

Is this God of Abram being righteous and just? Of course not, he should know that Abram got this richness by telling lies and deceiving Pharaoh.

Matthew 22:36-40

"Teacher, what are the greatest commandments in the Law?" Jesus replied, "Love the Lord your God with all your heart and with all your soul and with all your mind. This is the first greatest commandment. And the second is like it; Love your neighbour as yourself. All the law and the Prophets hang on these two commandments."

Abram was deceived by other gods who will put the souls in the darkness of sins. This is the reason why Abram and Sarai were trapped not to tell the truth. The promise of this Yahweh to Abram was not pure and holy for this was made known by being corrupt of not telling the truth. Abram put the soul of Pharaoh into trouble, because of the lies that Abram and Sara had to tell. Pharaoh took Sarai as his wife without knowing the truth that Sarai is the wife of Abram and not his sister, for this reason, the Pharaoh committed adultery.

Does Abram and Sarai did take good care of their souls and the soul of the Pharaoh?

Of course not, they did not care to love and respect their souls, which is why they were not able to love and respect the soul of Pharaoh. They put their souls into the darkness of sins. Abram and Sarai are great sinners who also put the soul of Pharaoh into trouble and sins that they had committed, for they both had corrupt minds and hearts.

Abram and Lot separate.

Genesis 13:7-12

A quarrel arose between the herdsmen of Abram's flock and those of Lot. (The Canaanites and the Perizzites were living in the land at that time.) Abram said to Lot, "Don't let there be a dispute between you and me, nor between my herdsmen and yours. Since we are brothers isn't the whole land there before you? Let us part company. If you go to the left, I will go to the right; if you go to the right, I will go to the left." Lot looked up and saw the whole valley of the Jordan: how well it was watered I before Yahweh destroyed Sodom and Gomorrah, this was like one of Yahweh's gardens, like the country of Egypt, on coming to Zoar. Lot chose for himself all the Jordan valley and journeyed eastward. In this way, they separated from each other. Abram settled in the country of Canaan while Lot lived among the towns of the plain and moved his tent as far as Sodom.

Before, Abram had nothing when he arrived in Egypt and met the Pharaoh. Abram and Sarai deceived the Pharaoh for not telling the truth. Abram received loads of mercy and blessings from the Pharaoh. The sheep, cattle, donkeys, menservants, maidservants, she-asses and camels. Then, afterwards, Pharaoh found out the truth that Abram and Sarai are husband and wife. Pharaoh just questioned Abram for not telling the truth and allowed him to take his wife and go. Pharaoh ordered his men about Abram, and they sent him his way, with his wife and all that was his.

A lot who went with Abram also had flocks, cattle and tents. The land was not sufficient to allow them to stay together because of which they separated. All the gifts that they had received from the Pharaoh separated them.

Genesis 13:14-18

Yahweh said to Abram after Lot had left him, "Raise your eyes and look from where you are, towards the north, the south, the east and the west; all the land you see I will give to you and your descendants forever. I will make your descendants as the dust of the earth; if the grains of the dust can be counted, then your descendants may be counted. Come, travel through the length and breadth of the land, for it is to you that I am giving it." So Abram moved his tent and came to live by the oak of Mamre at Hebron. There he built an altar to Yahweh.

1 John 2:15

Do not love the world or the things in the world. If anyone loves the world, the love of the Father is not in him.

Matthew 4:8-9

Then the devil took Jesus to a very high mountain, and showed him all the nations of the world in all their greatness and splendour. And he said, "All this I give to you, if you kneel down and worship me."

1 Corinthians 6: 19-20

Do you not know that your body is a temple of the Holy Spirit within you, given by God? You belong no longer to yourselves. Remember at what price you have been bought and make your body serve the glory of God.

The Yahweh of Abram is completely different from the God of Jesus. Abram accepted the offers of the richness of the world but Jesus rejected it. Abram built an altar for Yahweh. But for Jesus, the body is the temple of the Holy Spirit given by God, which means that our heart will be the centre and altar for the Lord. The altar that Abram built has no power to proclaim the words of God but through Jesus Christ, our body will be used for Godly purposes. We should need to use our body as the church for doing righteousness and just in the eyes of the Lord. Now it comes into my mind.

Is the Yahweh of Abram merciful, just and righteous?

I found not because the Yahweh of Abram is the deceiver who will lead one towards condemnation for the sake of the richness of this world. Who will mislead people not to love the Spirit of the Lord who is also living in the body of their brother and sister in the same image of our heavenly Father? What matters to Abram is to receive this richness of this world. The descendants of the family of Abram will continue to make sins, evil and create violence in the heart of others. This is the reason why it is said do not love the world or the things in the world. If anyone loves the world, the love of the Father is not in him. For Jesus knows that the kingdom of God and heaven is formed by Spirit which is you cannot see but it is the real source of life.

God's Covenant with Abram

(Genesis 15:1-5) After this the word of Yahweh was spoken to Abram in a vision; "Do not be afraid, Abram, I am your shield; your reward will be very great!" Abram said, "My Lord Yahweh, where are your promises? I am still childless and I have will go to Eliezer of Damascus. You have given me no children, so a slave of mine will be my heir." Then the word of Yahweh has spoken to him again, "Eliezer will not be your heir, but a child born of you (your own flesh and blood) will be your heir." Then Yahweh brought him outside and said to him, "Look up at the sky and count the stars if you can. Your descendants will be like that."

(Genesis 16:1-6) Sarai, Abram's wife, had not borne him a child, but she had an Egyptian servant named Hagar, and she said to Abram, "Now since Yahweh has kept me from having children, go to my servant; perhaps I shall have a child by her." Abram agreed to what Sarai said. Abram had been in the land of Canaan for ten years when Sarai, his wife, took Hagar, her Egyptian maid, and gave her husband as wife. He went into Hagar and she became pregnant. When she was aware of this, she began to despise her mistress. Sarai said to Abram, "May this injury done to me be yours. I put my servant in your arms and now that she knows she is pregnant, I count for nothing in her eyes. Let Yahweh judge between me and you." Abram said to Sarai, "Your servant is in your power; do with her as you please." Then Sarai treated her so badly that she ran away.

I am just wondering what kind of God does Abram have? Why this one is so mean? He allows Abram to commit more sins.

- Abram's words are full of lies.

1. He deceived Pharaoh for not telling the truth and made Pharaoh be a sinner by committing adultery to his wife.

2. He did not accept his wrong-doing to be corrected for not telling the truth, instead, he received gifts from Pharaoh.
3. He got separated from Lot for the sake of the riches
4. He listened to Sarai to take Hagar as his mistress. He knows that he is committing adultery.
5. He allows Sarai to maltreat Hagar.

- God's promises to Abram;

1. I will make you a great nation.
2. I will bless you and make your name great, and you will be a blessing.
3. I will bless those who bless you, and whoever curses you, I will curse, and in you, all people of the earth will be blessed.
4. Raise your eyes and look from where you are, towards the north, the south, the east and the west; all the land you see. I will give to you and your descendants forever.
5. Do not be afraid, Abram I am your shield; your reward will be very great.
6. Look up at the sky and count the stars if you can, your descendants will be like that.

Abram's work did not show mercy, love and compassion to the soul of others. He works for himself and does what pleases him and the Spirit. He kept on being corrupt by not telling the truth and walking disobediently to what is not right to the Spirit.

Genesis 9: 3-6

Everything that moves and lives shall be food for you; as I gave you the green plants, I have now given you everything. Only you shall not eat flesh with its life that is its blood. But I will also demand a reckoning for your lifeblood, I will demand it from every animal, and a man too. I will demand a reckoning for the life of his fellowman. He who shed the blood of man shall have his bloodshed by man; for in the image of God has made man.

God has given only two different kinds of gender between humans and animals. Remember we are only travellers in this world and have been given only a limited amount of time to journey with the Spirit that has been bestowed upon us. Therefore, if you reject the truth and choose what pleases to your flesh once you depart from this world your soul will be in terrible reckoning that you deserved. Remember that our lifeblood came from the same God in the realm of the Spirit. God is a Spirit and our soul is the source of our lifeblood that will be put into judgement according to our deeds. If you knew that you are created to be a man stand yourself as God you created you to be a man same as well as a woman if God formed you as a woman live in this way and don't ever think you can mock God for he is the truth and he knows what is truthful and righteous to His eyes.

Lust is a temptation and evil that is born in Satan's strategies to condemn the souls of many. The body, however, is not meant for sexual immorality for this is for the Lord to be the temple for truthfulness and righteousness that will lead to our soul to walk in Spirit of dignity, integrity and morality.

Psalm 101:3

I will not look with approval on anything that is vile. I hate what faithless people do I will have no part in it.

Exodus 20:14

You shall not commit adultery.

Matthew 5:28

But I tell you that anyone who looks at a woman lustfully has already committed adultery with her in his heart.

1 John 2:16

For everything in the world—the lust of the flesh, the lust of the eyes, and the pride of life—comes not from the Father but the world.

James 1:14-15

But each person is tempted when they are dragged away by their own evil desire and enticed.

Then after desire has conceived, it gives birth to sin; and sin, when it is full-grown, gives birth to death.

When your heart's desire inclines to do that what pleases your flesh your soul which is the innocent image and child of God that is living within you and which is giving life to your body is not free and healthy for this is cast in the hell of death of pain, crying and suffering because lust was come from Satan's strategies to put one masterpiece of God in death.

Galatians 5:16

So I say, walk by the Spirit and you will not gratify the desires of the flesh.

Romans 8:6

The mind governed by the flesh is death, but the mind governed by the Spirit is life and peace.

The Reality of the Present World

Our world is broken and still living in hypocrisy because of the lies and strategies of Satan. Sins are still in higher possession to put and ruining each soul. Most children of God have lost their inheritance of eternal life because they are sinners. It is easy for many to love Satan, and not to love and obey God.

Matthew 7:13

Enter through the narrow gate. For wide is the gate and broad is the road that leads to destruction, and many enter through it.

Matthew 7:14

But small is the gate and narrow the road that leads to life and only a few find it.

Jesus Is the Greatest Hope for Eternal Life

Who Is John the Baptist?

(John 1:6-9)

A man came, sent by God; his name was John. He came to bear witness, to introduce the Light so that all might believe through him. He was not the Light but a witness to introduce the Light. For the light was coming into the world, the true Light that enlightens everyone.

John is the son of Elisabeth and Zechariah. Both of them belonged to priestly families. Even at very old ages, God blessed them with a child because they were both innocent in the eyes of God and lived blamelessly in accordance with all the laws and commands of the Lord. Angel Gabriel firstly appeared to Zechariah to speak and bring good news.

Angel Gabriel Appeared To Mary

In the sixth month, the Angel Gabriel was sent by God to a town of Galilee called Nazareth. He was sent to a young virgin, who was betrothed to a man named Joseph, of the family of David; and the virgin's name was Mary.

The angel came to her and said, "Rejoice, full of grace, the Lord is with you." Mary was troubled at these words, wondering what this greeting could mean. But the angel said, "Do not fear, Mary, for God has looked kindly on you. You shall conceive and bear a son, and you shall call him Jesus. He will be great and shall rightly be called Son of the Highest. And His reign shall have no end."

Then Mary said to the Angel, "How can this be since I am a virgin?"

Angel Gabriel said, "And the Holy Spirit will come upon you and the power of the Highest will overshadow you; therefore, the Holy Child to be born of you shall be called Son of God. Even your relative Elisabeth is expecting a son in her old age, although she was unable to have a child. And she is now in her sixth month. With God nothing is impossible."

Then Mary said, "I am the handmaid of the Lord, let it be done to me as you have said." And the angel left her.

In the Gospel of Matthew 4:4

Jesus said, "One does not live by bread alone, but on every word that comes 'from the mouth of God'."

The world was created from the words of God. Every creation is formed supernaturally from the presence of the Spirit of the Lord. In everything that we see with our eyes was created and evolving with one Spirit of the Lord, Who has the power to give life. This will prove that humans will not be able to stand alone without the presence of the Spirit of the Lord. It is the Spirit who gives life to move our being. It is true that humans are from dust and will be turned again to dust.

Every living creature that we have ever seen has limited time to live because it is only temporary. From then I understand that humans are only travellers in this world. We all have been given the life to live and explore in this world which is heaven if we teach ourselves to walk and live by Spirit and lean on God and not on our own understanding. But because of pride, people are more rovers of the richness of the world and turned this planet into hell rather than a paradise.

The story of the life of Elisabeth and Zechariah was formed as they were both walking upright in the laws of God. At their old age, they can't bear a child but because God found that they were both upright in the eyes of the Lord God blessed them to have a child miraculously. Through them was first formed that nothing is impossible for God. In human understanding how this can be? Through them was born a child named John and who would later be called John the Baptist.

Mary was a simple woman with a pure heart. She was chosen by God so that Jesus is born in the world. Even though she was troubled deep within her heart and questioning how this can happen, for she is a virgin. It was then, as a second thought that nothing is impossible with God. Jesus was conceived in the womb of Mary by the Holy Spirit.

Throughout his life, Jesus was guided by the Holy Spirit and He led his life as a true and exact representation of the personality of God.

Jesus' Story Before He Met John the Baptist

When Jesus was born, his earthly parents encountered such great trouble in life how they will protect Jesus from not being killed for a king named Herod was jealous of him. An angel of the Lord appeared in a dream to Joseph and said, "Get up, take the child and his mother and flee to Egypt and stay there until I tell you, for Herod will soon be looking for the child in order to kill him." Joseph got up, took the child and his mother, and left that night for Egypt, where he stayed until the death of Herod.

John the Baptist was born to bear witness to introduce Jesus as a Messiah and Son of the Highest. John the Baptist will baptise people by water; he preached a baptism of repentance for the forgiveness of sins. He knows in his heart that there is one who is greater than him that will baptise people by the Holy Spirit.

Knowing Jesus' life story by heart is a gift of representing who is God for us. At the young age of 12, he expressed some wisdom to the elders in the temple about God. His mother Mary and former father Joseph were searching for him and they found that Jesus was sitting among the teachers, listening to them and asking questions. And all the people were amazed at his understanding and his answers. Jesus was filled with wisdom and the grace of God was upon him.

In the Gospel of Luke 2: 48-50

It is written saying that, His parents were very surprised when they saw him, and his mother said to him, "Son, why have you done this to us?" In reply, Jesus said, "Why were you looking for me? Did you not know that I must be in my Father's house?" But they did not understand this answer.

Honestly, we were not able to understand that response if we didn't get to the point of what is in the mind and the desire of the heart of Jesus.

As we can see in the story of Mary before she conceived Jesus in her womb, Angel Gabriel was come upon her saying that he was sent from God to tell Mary that God has looked kindly on her and not to be fear for she shall conceive and bear a son by the Holy Spirit. The angel Gabriel told Mary that she will call him Jesus. He will be great and shall rightly be called Son of the Highest. And His reign shall have no end.

The revelation of our existence is completely different from Jesus. A man and women need to be one before they conceive another life. But what had happened to Marv was different. No wonder Mary questioned Angel Gabriel for she is a virgin.

Joseph the carpenter is the former father of Jesus. Through blood, he is not the real father of Jesus. The Holy Spirit is the father of Jesus. And this is the reason why John the Baptist said that there is one greater than him. Because he knew that Jesus is the chosen one of God that will help people to baptise by the Holy Spirit.

Mary did not understand that Jesus is initiating to people who is God. Ask you can see, Jesus did not call Mary his mother. He called her woman. For Jesus, his parent does not come from this world but the omnipresent One who is the founder and creator of all life and that is the Holy Spirit. And this is the reason why Jesus also said that the unforgivable sins are when you slandered the Holy Spirit.

Jesus is the only begotten son of the Lord. He was sent by God from heaven but forms as a human from the flesh of Mary. Jesus is a true servant of the Lord, through him the love of the Almighty Father will be revealed to us. Jesus is the

'LIGHT, the WAY, and the TRUTH'. He is the Messiah that will baptise people to repentance so that every soul will be led by the gift of the Holy Spirit. And from then a person who was born by the flesh will be born again as a new creation of God by the Holy Spirit.

In every moment of their lives, the Holy Trinity will govern their soul out of sins. Satan has no more power to manipulate, harm and kill one soul because Jesus is alive in their hearts. The time we received the gift from Jesus we received God. Through Jesus, we can also conquer the grave. Our soul will be out of death and in our hearts, God is our guidance in every moment of our life. And from then, we always put God first in our lives and lean on His understanding. We will understand that our home is in the arms of God for we are called to his childlike as Jesus. This world that we live now was to an end once God has taken away the life that has given to us. Our journey to this world is finished therefore I understood that we don't have a future in this world because our future will depend on how we give great respect and care to the Spirit that is living within us while we still live and exist into this world. All people will be judge according to our deeds.

Jesus said that our body is the temple of the Lord. He gave as the two greatest commandments first, to love God with all our heart, mind and soul with all our strength and secondly is to love our neighbours as ourselves.

We were not able to perform that without knowing who is God in our heart and His personality. Jesus said that no one can ever see or hear God. He said that God is a Spirit. He thought as an example of the wind. We were not able to see the wind but we were able to tell in which part may come from.

In Psalm 34:18 said,

When you are broken-hearted, am close to you.

God is always with us even we are broken-hearted that is the very moment He was waiting and looking upon on to our heart to call Him as our greatest helper in times of troubles.

But because we are not aware to ourselves that there is someone omnipresent who is the greatest of all who are always with us if we seek Him for help to lean on but we human beings, our problems is we always choose to solve our problems by itself and seek some help to others who are not also aware to our problems and at the end we are more leads to confusion and misguided because we allow others to decide for ourselves.

Honestly, God is our greater encourager if we allow Him to govern our life. We are His masterpiece of His Spirit through Him we live and move our being. He knows everything about us because He is the creator of our life, the Alpha and Omega.

God said if you will seek me with all your heart you will find me and I will reveal myself to you. Knowing the personality of God, who He is, and what He wants for us is a form and foundation of faith.

From then we were able to transform ourselves as a new creation of God. Love and forgiveness will burn inside us like a flame into our hearts. We can understand the purpose of life and the meaning of it. We were able to forgive ourselves and love our enemies. The truth will come to realise and be understood as well.

Honestly, our greatest enemy is our ego. Because of this, we are trap in troubles and heartaches that will lead to a relationship being broken. And because of this most people are lost and carrying the unforgiving Spirit into their heart, the love is dead and if the love is still there it is covered by hatred, anger, grudge and bitterness no wonder we don't have peace and happiness into our hearts because our soul is in the darkness of sins.

Jesus said that God hates pride, the reason why is because pride is boastful and are not being able to love and forgive. This is the reason why the world is broken because most people are contaminated of this sickness that will lead to a person not to love and forgive.

Jesus said that God is a spirit to whom you cannot see but He is the giver of life. Through Him, the world was formed and has been created.

Jesus said that a man should not live alone with bread. Honestly, the truth is every living thing that you will ever see has its own life because the power of God is universal and we will find it everywhere. Through that, we live and move our being. Our soul is the masterpiece of the Spirit of God who is living within us. Without that Spirit, our body won't have fife. To tell that food is not the main source that will give us life to our body but most are our soul is the one who gives our body to fife which is completely neglected to care for being love and respect.

In 1 Corinthians 6:19-20 said,

Do you not know that your body is a temple of the Holy Spirit within you, given by God? You belong no longer to yourselves. Remember at what price you have been bought and make your body serve the Glory of God.

Honestly, the miracle of life was made from the evolutions of the Holy Spirit. Jesus was formed with the Holy Spirit before the annunciation to Mary. Jesus is the only begotten child of God that will baptise people in the Holy Spirit. This is the reason the believers and followers of Jesus Christ will receive the gift of the Holy Spirit which is;

Wisdom—let us judge things in the way that God does.

Understanding—the gift that helps us to understand all God has told us.

Right Judgement—this gift help us to know what to do especially when faced with really difficult situations.

Courage—this gives us the strength to do what is right no matter how hard.

Knowledge—lets us see the world as it is. Reverence—this gift gives us the power to love God and our neighbour as we should.

Wonder and Awe in God's Presence—this gives us the power to remember the greatness of God and consequently gives us a horror of offending God who has loved us so much.

Love, joy, peace, patience, kindness, gentleness and self-control are the fruits of the Holy Spirit in our lives once we received the gift of Jesus. This is the reason why God said, "When you received the gift of my son Jesus you received me?"

Jesus said that our body is the temple of the Lord but for many, they transformed it into a grave because of their sins. Now how can we say and perform that we love God if we refuse to ourselves to love the Holy Spirit who is Jiving within into our body by turning our body into the grave of our sins rather than being kept as the temple of the Lord for Godly purposes?

Jesus commands us to love one another. How can we ever do that? If we still have the marked by the beast. Honestly, pride is the mark of the beast that is living also in all human hearts. It is the pride who governs one heart to turn evil not to love one another. By pride, all souls are in the darkness of sins.

In the Gospel of Matthew 7:13-14 said;

Enter through the narrow gate; for wide is the gate and broad is the road that leads to destruction, and many go that way. How narrow is the gate that leads to life, and how rough the road; few there are who find it.

Jesus thought us to repent and sin no more for he knows that the wages of sin are death. But for many, they would rather more to commit sins than to repent and sin no more. Because most people are not aware that sins are the one who has the power to kill both the body and soul that will throw your life into the fires of hell. Most people in this world choose what really pleases to their flesh and not to their Spirit who is not seen but has giving life to their flesh. They don't see and understand that their life comes from the Spirit who is living within them and not on by the flesh itself alone.

We have given only a temporary life, for we are only travellers in this world. Our times here on earth is only temporary. Jesus thought us so to be on guard and get ready. This means that we should cleanse our soul by repenting from our sins so that our sins will be forgiven and then when the times will come that we are going to depart in this world our soul is ready to face for the time of judgement. Every soul is important to God. This is the reason why God sent Jesus, His only begotten son to this world so that through Him we were able to with the presence of God.

Genesis 2:2-3

By the seventh day the work God had done was completed, and He rested on the seventh day from all the work He had done. And God blessed the seventh day and made it Holy because on that day he rested from all the work he had done in His creation.

John 1:17

For the law was given to Moses; grace and truth came through Jesus.

Mark 2:27

Then Jesus said to them, The Sabbath was made for man, not man for Sabbath.

Jesus has wisdom and knowledge of understanding that Sabbath is been made for people to relax, rested and enjoy ourselves after our works is been done. Sabbath is not about telling us not to move our body, not to work ourselves what makes us happy but do what makes you feel happy, peaceful and content not only for our own interest but also to others who really in need of our help. Sabbath is to form ourselves to do good and rested, not to put ourselves to be angry and stressed about being negative because of not following Moses' law.

For Moses, Sabbath is a law of saying no to work. So if you did not keep this commandment to make it Holy. It means if you work on Sabbath, yourself will be put to stone to death. For Moses, this is unforgivable sins. But for Jesus, it is a way only of relaxing yourself and loving the Spirit who is living within your body.

Jesus did not obey and listen to this commandment of Moses. For this reason, Jesus is criticised, persecuted and hated by others. Jesus has the full knowledge of the personality of our Almighty Father therefore God sent Jesus to the world to baptise all humankind in the power of the Holy Spirit and the love of God for us will be revealed through Jesus Christ. Moses has given more Laws to deceived people to keep in mind to have the promised-land and not to have the inheritance of eternal life. Moses' life is not led by the Holy Spirit no wonder he is being misled by giving the favour and sight what will please the flesh rather than the Spirit.

In the Old Testament, the Ten Commandments are given to Moses. And the God of Moses added more law in this commandment which is Jesus tried to correct it with the justice of truth. The words and scriptures of Jesus are formed and led by the Holy Spirit, therefore, the truth is been revealed and set to people to live and walk by the Spirit if you managed to yourself to seek in God heartedly.

Jesus is a living sacrifice for the souls of many. He is been put to the cross because he corrected the Ten Commandments of Moses and makes it only into the Two greatest commandments. In these real times, many are still blind about the truth. Those people are still believing Moses' law and through the God of Abraham and Noah. Many souls are been still a loss because of these corrupt words to this prophet. Therefore anyone who will believe in Jesus will not get the Promised Land that the Lord of Moses was talking to but will inherit the eternal life.

Part-Two
Mystery and Beauty of Life

Gospel of Luke 4:4

But Jesus answered, "Scriptures says: People cannot live on bread alone."

Jesus is being tempted in the wilderness to the test by the devil. After spending forty days and forty nights without food, Jesus is hungry. Jesus is full of wisdom. He was really sure and confident about his answer. He knows that man lives by the Holy Spirit who's living in their bodies and not only by food. He is confident to tell Satan that the true nature of the life of a person depends on the Spirit and not by food alone. As we can see a person who has not Spirit in his /her body has no life and purpose at all for their bodies are dead and must be buried into the grave. Most people of God are lost because of a lack of knowledge, not knowing where their existence comes from.

Now in these days most people are lost and are still blind not knowing this Knowledge. Some are stressing themselves what pleases their flesh not realising that it is the Holy Spirit that has given the source to us to live and move our being. Most people depend on money. Some people wondered if they have more money they can live in a more pleasing and peaceful life. They don't realise and recognised that money has no power over God because money cannot create and provide one soul and the other.

Many people believe, "It's my body, and I can treat it anyway I like." But what does our Creator God say? 1 Corinthians 3:17 said, "If anyone destroys God's temple, God will destroy that person; for God's temple is sacred, and you are that temple." Even though God has given us the free will to live and journey ourselves as per our desires we should know and understand that we are not in superior for our lives but God is, because He is the source of everything, our soul is only a masterpiece of His being. He is the Alpha and Omega, the beginning and the end. This is the reason why it is said, you cannot serve two Masters you will love the one and hate the other. You cannot serve both God and money.

Mystery and beauty of life have revealed in the wisdom by the intimates love letter from God. "Here I will share to expand my understanding about the true nature and value of life." My experience thought me so and I am happy to share it to others. May the Holy Spirit bestow also you the wisdom to have the grace, mercy and compassion towards to yourself and to others by loving your neighbours as yourself.

Acts 17:28

In me, you live and move and have your being.

We are all created from the same image of God. Jesus said that God is a Spirit and no one can ever hear or see God. Jesus explains example to us that God really exists like as the form of the wind. We were not able to see it by our sight but our heart has the vision to see and understand the one is invisible, we can tell that the wind can really exist. Our soul is the Spirit that comes from God who lives in our body. Through our soul, God is familiar with all our ways. He knows about everything us because God lives in us. We cannot hide anything from God because our soul is the string that will attach ourselves to God and our boarding pass to the gate of heaven. Our soul is the offspring that God is referring to us that we are connected to Him. Everything that we do and even what is in our heart and mind we cannot hide it away to God.

God gave us the gift of conscience, through this we can say if we are walking obediently to God or not. It is our conscience who can tell and judge us if we did wrong and we turn against God. Through our conscience, we can reflect for everything that we have done from the past and seek to find our way back to the Lord our Almighty Father. Our heart and mind will be set to repentance and asking for forgiveness of the Lord. From then our conscience and the Holy Spirit will lead and guide us to the way that we should go.

We are a new creation of God. The gift of the Holy Spirit will be bestowed upon us to walking obediently and living by the Spirit. Our soul is our major interest and priority for our lives because we will find that our soul is the source of our lives that will bring us to inherit the eternal life that Jesus has promised.

John 8: 41-44

I have been misrepresented by those who don't know me.

Honestly, religion in this world has the greatest impact on all. Through this most people are being hypocrites. This is the reason why Jesus told that not everyone who says to me, 'Lord, Lord,' will enter the kingdom of heaven, but the one who does the will of my Father who is in heaven. As we can see most people who belong to the congregation of their religion are having a comparison towards each other. They were found criticising each other just only for the sake of the names and titles of their religion. Now religion is being used for making money this is the reality of what's going on, most Christians are been baptised by water but not by the Holy Spirit. No wonder many hearts of a person in the Christian religion is living in hypocrisy.

Religions in this world cannot help us to save our soul unless we received the mystery of the gift of the Holy Spirit. We should be baptised and born again by the Holy Spirit through Jesus Christ. In Jesus, the love of the Lord for us will be revealed in him. He is the exact representation of God's personality. Having the wisdom to understand what is in the mind and the desire of the heart of Jesus is the greatest gift that anyone can have. It is a precious treasure that no one can ever take away from you but you can multiply also to the lives of others by helping to persuade them too, also to walk and live by Spirit.

God is the Alpha and Omega, the beginning and the end. Each one of us has given the life to live from the time that we are born and will end once we depart in this world. We have given only the times to travel in this world. This is the reason why Jesus said that his kingdom is not here on earth but in heaven for he knows that our home is revealed on Spirit which is you cannot see but has the power to exist supernaturally. But in this world where we live, Satan has the power to deceived and manipulate peoples heart and peoples mind by offering the richness of the world which is Jesus rejected because Jesus knows that the things from the world do not belong to God and we cannot bring that to the place where our soul should go after our times has ended to travel in this world. This is also the reason why Jesus said we cannot serve two masters. We will love the one and hate the other. Because the truth is we were not able to serve both money and God.

Psalm 139:1

You may not know me, but I know everything about you.

Jesus said that God is a Spirit. Therefore God knows us by our Spirit. Our soul is the foundation of our life that is freely given to us by God and through that, we are connected to Him. All humans must know themselves as a child of God by Spirit and not by flesh or any title that comes from the world. This is the reason why God sent Jesus his only begotten son to this world so that through him we were able to see the kingdom of God. (Luke 12:54-56) He said to the crowd, "When you see a cloud rising in the west, immediately you say, 'It's going to rain', and it does. And when the south wind blows, you say, 'It's going to be hot' and it is." Hypocrites, You know how to interpret the appearance of the earth and the sky. How is it that you don't know how to interpret this present time? Jesus was telling to us that if will seek upon on the kingdom of God we can know to understand that Heaven is here now. This world is still the same paradise that is been created by God when He created the world. But because of Satan, the world was doomed by sins. Satan interferes the human's heart to going rebellious to God therefore humans are been blind about the truth. They lose their light that is why they lack in knowing which one will give favour to God. Jesus came to this world to be the light of the world so that through him our soul will be enlightened again and renew our mind to which one is important and pleasing to God. Jesus did not come to save the flesh but he came to save the souls out from sin. This is the reason why He said blessed are those who have not seen and yet have believed. Jesus came to the world to help people to walk and live by the grace of the Spirit because the truth is man is from dust and the dust returns to the ground it came from, and the Spirit returns to God who gave it. (Matthew 10:28) Do not be afraid of those who kill the body but cannot kill the soul. Rather be afraid of the One who can destroy both soul and body in hell. (Romans 6:23) For the wage of sins is death, but the gift of God is eternal life in Christ Jesus our Lord. Sins are from the strategies of Satan to deceived people to put their soul in darkness of hell of sins of pain, crying and suffering this is the reason why Jesus is calling to everyone's heart to repent and sin no more because the wages of sins will be death for each soul as the child of God. Through repentance, we can resurrect our soul again as the child of God. Holy Spirit is the one who will lead our lives to journey our days by the presence of the Lord. Peace, love, happiness and joy will shine upon on our heart. No one can ever steal from us or ruin it by rust or moth. For it is securely safe in the hands of the Lord our soul is saved and have the place to inherit the eternal life. Satan will try to give all his tactics to deceive the child of God but he will not succeed because the Holy Spirit is in-charge now to govern the heart, mind and soul of His child. They will stand by their Faith walking obediently to God. They will keep their body as the temple of the Lord and not by putting it as the grave for their sins. They know deep within their heart that if they will go back to please their flesh and not the Spirit they will know that their soul will be in great torment. Repentance can be done only while we still exist in this world and not once the Spirit is been rip out from our body for this will be too late.

Jeremiah 1:4-5

I knew you even before you were conceived.

How Jesus has come to this world was come from the mind and grace of the Holy Spirit. We human beings were also come as well by the mind and grace of the Holy Spirit. We evolve on this planet because of the Holy Spirit. The life that is given and bestowed to us has come from the same power of the Holy Spirit this is the reason we have the life to travel and journey into this planet. Adam was formed by the clay God gave breath from his nostril therefore Adam turns his body to life. It is simply understood that the very essence and source of life comes from the Spirit of the Lord which is you cannot see but has giving magic to live supernaturally. Our soul is the offspring of God these is the string that will say and prove that we are connected to the very source of our Almighty Father. Every single lie is not hidden to Him. He knows from our very heart what we have done to ourselves and others. Nothing will be hidden to God because he knows the desire and intentions of our works. God can differentiate if what we have done is evil or not that will make harm to our soul. This is the reason why God said I am familiar with all your ways because He knows everything about us. He allows us to see the wonders of all creation by journeying and travelling in this world. We are all fearfully and wonderfully made by His figure of his Spirit. He determined the exact time of our birth and when it will last longer to live ourselves to journey but in this world because of the people who are evil in their heart they choose to create weapons to kill the body so that these souls have no more chances to journey in this world. Some souls is been wasted and in great suffering because of lust. In Africa, there are so many innocent child loss their chances to live peacefully because grown-up is acting like a beast for the sake of lust. Many child are not been look after as they should and their governments are not helping how to give support to live people in procrastination with perseverance to care this innocent child. The Lord has been blamed for this, some people were questioning God why he allows it to happen. It is Satan's strategy to hurt the souls of many and not God. If we could understand that we are only travellers in this world that one day we will depart because our body is from dust and this will return to dust and our soul will go back to where it belongs for this is not belong to this world but it belongs in the kingdom of God which is in Heaven. But because of the sins, souls are in great danger of troubles of pain, crying and suffering and this is the necklace for every unholy deed that we apply and created into our life. This is the reason why Jesus is calling every one's heart to repent and sin no more because the wages of sins is death for the souls of the sinner. Our body was formed as the temple of the Lord and not the grave for our sins. Therefore we should keep it Holy for morality and only God's purposes and not to what makes will please to Satan.

Psalm 139:15-16

You were not a mistake for all your days are written in my book.

Our Almighty Father bestowed upon us the part of His Spirit so that we may be able to journey and travel in this world. He created us with His love in our mother's womb. Therefore a new child of God which is pure and innocent will be born in this world. God brings us to the world for having a purpose to love and be love but the world is not the same paradise as God created from the beginning. Satan got to have access to deceive all the child of God and then loss their inheritance of eternal life. Most souls of children of God have been contaminated by sins, these are the reason why the world is broken and formed by never-ending pain and suffering. God already sent his only begotten son Jesus so that through him we will find our purpose to journey with the presence of the Lord in every day of our life. But it is not easy to understand the God ways because you will be put to the test in fires of trials and heartaches before you understand it. It is said that God is very close to the broken-hearted. I found that it is true because I experience it. God said if you will seek me with all your heart, you will find me and I will reveal myself to you. From then I have a different perspective and point of view about life. I found that this world is the same paradise that God has created before. Heaven is here now when you learn to walk and live by Spirit. You were not afraid for you will understand that you have given only a limited time to journey in this world and God knows when he will come back to take away the life that he bestowed upon us. Now in every task that I should do my thoughts and my hearts are always connected to God. I put my soul as my greatest priority because I know that at the end of my days my soul will come to face the time of Judgement according to how I took good care to love the Spirit of God who is living into my body. Jesus said that our body is the temple of the Lord. The first commandment is to love God with all your heart, your mind, and your soul with all your strength. How can we ever do that if we haven't the knowledge to know the personality of God? For humans understanding, it is impossible to do it but for God nothing is impossible. This is the reason why God said my thoughts are not your thoughts therefore our understanding is not the same like as our Almighty Father. It is said to lean on God and not on our own understanding. How can we ever make it happen to get to know what is in the mind of God if we haven't understood what is the desire of His heart? Only through Jesus and real repentance we are able to be baptised by the Holy Spirit. And from then the Holy Spirit is the one who will lead our life to go to the way that we should go. Peace, joy and happiness are planted into our hearts. Satan has no more power to hurt and kill our soul.

1 John 4:16

I am not distant and angry, but I am the complete expressions of love.

Jesus said that our body is the temple of the Lord. From there it comes into my mind and heart that God is always with us. Even we make mistakes he always forgives us. His unconditional love is big and wide. He wants us to know that in every trouble we have face He is in there also but we can't see him because we are blind about His personality. Even we always choose to commit sins. He is always extending our days to learn and seek his forgiveness but most people are getting more upset and confused because of Satan and ended being more rebellious to God. God is always giving us the chances to seek him and his righteousness so that we may gain His love and born again as a new creation of God. But it is said that God will come in the night like as a theft no one can ever know what time He will come. Therefore, we should be in guard and get ready to put our heart into repentance so that our soul will be cleansed again as a pure and innocent child in the eyes of the Lord. But if a sinner did not keep his or her body as a temple of the Lord again they will be cast out from heaven their soul will be in torment. God wants us to journey our days by walking and living with His presence so that our soul will be happy in peace, satisfied and content. We have been called as the child of the Lord because of our soul and not by our flesh or the title that we are carrying into this world. Our souls belong to the kingdom of God and not here on earth. A Spirit (soul) belongs to the realm of the Spirit. But our flesh was from dust and this will return to dust for this is where belong to.

Matthew 7:11

I offer you more than your earthly father ever could.

Our earthly parents must only an instrument for God therefore through them another child of God will be born to the world. Our earthly parents are also called as a child of God and be considered as our neighbours who are also living to this world temporarily. Their life is also equally like to anyone for we are only like aliens and travellers in this world. No one man in this world has proven to live eternally even the prophets are gone. For these reasons, we do not belong to anyone in this world. Each one of us has lost our knowledge that our home does not belong into this world and we have only one invisible parent that come from the same image in the realm of Spirit and has bestowed our life to journey into this world and that is in the presence of the Spirit of our Almighty Father. This is the reason why Jesus did not recognise Mary and Joseph as his parents because, for him, his real and perfect Father is the One who sent him which is invisible to the sight of many.

Luke 2:41-52

Every year the parents of Jesus went to Jerusalem for the feast of the Passover, as was customary. And when Jesus was twelve years old, he went with them, according to the custom of this feast. After the festival was over, they returned, but the boy Jesus remained in Jerusalem, and his parents did not know it. They thought he was in the company, and after walking the whole day they looked for him among their relatives and friends. As they did not find him, they went back to Jerusalem searching for him, and on the third day, they found him in the Temple, sitting among the teachers, listening to them and asking questions. And all the people were amazed at his understanding and his answers. His parents were very surprised when they saw him, and his mother said to him, "Son, why have you done this to us? Your father and I were very worried while searching for you."

Then he said to them, "Why were you looking for me? Did you not know that I must be in my Father's house? But they did not understand this answer."

Jesus went down with them, returning to Nazareth, and he continued to be subject to them. As for his mother, she kept all these things on her heart. And Jesus increased in wisdom and age, and in the divine in human favour.

Although Mary and Joseph knew much about Jesus, full understanding had not yet dawned. Jesus was both human and divine for he was knitted by the Holy Spirit together in Mary's womb. Arc Angel Gabriel announced that Jesus would be called the Son of the Highest and His Kingdom will last forever. For parental concern, Mary and Joseph were anxious in searching for Jesus because God trusted them to be as a guardian and earth angel who will look after to Jesus to journey on this world. But Jesus was totally preoccupied with His interest in Spiritual matters. Jesus grew in stature and strength, and was filled with wisdom; the grace of God was upon him. God loves us more than from our earthly father because the source of everything that we have received comes from God who is the Father of all souls. God said that he lives within us and he is familiar in all our ways because He is the one who will sustain us to journey with His presence in every day of our life. As long as God is giving us a day to journey in this world He will be always with us. But because of the pandemic disease that is been marked to the hearts of many, we ruined and put our souls into the death of pain, crying and suffering. The only way to set again to be purified and cleanse our soul to be free is to seek in for forgiveness to the Lord by putting our heart into repentance. Sins are the pandemic disease and the wage of this is death which is not easily cured no wonder the world is broken and every child of God is been loss.

Jeremiah 29:11

My plan for your future has always been filled with hope.
As we all know that God is the Alpha and Omega our life in this world has also the beginning and an end. We have given the privilege to journey our days to see the wonders of God and how marvellous is His work. God hopes for us that even we travelled in this world our heart mind and soul will still be connected in His heart so that we may enjoy our journey while we travel in this world. One day He will come back to us to end our days on this planet for we do not belong to this world but our soul which is our lifeblood from God will return to Him. The problem in this world Satan has interacted between the bonding of God and His child. Satan deceived humanities heart and mind to be unlawful to God and from then the world has never-ending war and violence. Because of this, the paradise that God has created was formed by as the battlefield between good and evil. God sent Jesus as our brother in Spirit that will give us light and hope to go back to the Lord. He is the chosen one and the Messiah that will lead people to walk and live by Spirit but because humanities are blind about truth, because of the pride most people are being hard-headed because their mind is not open yet to accept God as their real Father who will love them unconditionally who

will sustain and provide us everything if we go deeper to know His understanding. Even we are given only limited times to live most people are so focused on gaining to have the richness in this world for the future. But I found that in this troubled world we don't have a future for our future must be secured only by our Spirit. Our soul is our key to the gate of heaven but these souls will be judge according to our deeds. How did we act to love and respect these Spirit who is living within us, God wants us all for the very best but we cannot have it if we will choose to what will give pleasures to our flesh and not to the Spirit. God wants us all to take our days to journey with His presence by walking and living by Spirit for this is the only way we can be fully happy, content and satisfied to be in peace all the time in our life. And when the times He will come back we are ready and happy to depart and be thankful to God our Almighty Father for having the chances and privilege to travel in this world.

Matthew 6:31–33

For I am your provider and I meet all your needs.

God is the source of everything. He prepared this world as a paradise as also a place and home for every child of God (souls) to travel in this world. This is the reason why God said every good gift that you received comes from my hand. Before we ask He already knows what we need that is why before He created man and human in this world everything is freely given to them to govern and eat aside only from the fruit of the tree of knowledge between good and evil. Because God knows that this tree of knowledge between good and evil is contaminated by the mark of the beast and once you eat it your soul which is your life will be going to be dead. But Adam and Eve was been deceived by Satan that is why they eat the fruit and from then generations in so many generations of souls until now are been confused by the tactics of Satan. People are more loving to the richness of the world. Humans are from dust and this will return to dust but in our world of full of sins, people choose always to give a favour on what pleases their lust. Prostitute, pornography, adultery are the cases of sins that is into the society so that Satan's can have access to ruin more souls to be drowned in sins. Jesus said you cannot serve two masters. You will love the one and hate the other. You cannot serve both God and money. Prostitute and pornography work for the sake of money these will favour for lust. Adultery is both connected on being prostitute and pornography the fruit of work is lustfully pleasing to the flesh and not to the Spirit. God said my plan for your future has always been filled with hope. God is not distant or angry with us. He understands that His child is been loss because of lack of knowledge. God's plan for us for the future is always been filled with hope that one day we may put our heart to seek Him and ask for His forgiveness and from then we will cleanse to purify our soul again to be called as a child of God. Our lifeblood (soul) from God is renewed to walk and live by the presence of the Spirit which is formed by One Holy Trinity. This is the reason why Jesus said that I and the Father are one because their purpose is to save the souls out from purgatory. Many people are dead because of sins but once a person seeks on God and puts their heart to repentance God will bestow you the wisdom that you belong to Him and He will raise you out from the dead. Through your deep repentance, God was rejoicing and singing that my child has been a loss but then he/ she is been found. And the soul of a child of God will have the power to move the mountains of problems and not be shaken for the Faith that they have is been planted in their mind, heart and soul with all God's strength. Their souls will fly like eagles and not worry for the Lord our loving God is in our side. To whom shall I be afraid, deep in your heart you will feel great confidence. If God is for me no one man can ever be against me.

Jeremiah 31:3

Because I love you with an everlasting love.

God is the Alpha and Omega. He writes our names into His book of life. He loves us more than our earthly father. He is a loving, merciful and compassionate Father of all. His love is unconditional and unwavering. He always understands us and always forgives even we are hurting Him so many times. Jesus said that our body is the temple of the Lord but as human beings, because of lack of knowledge we broke our body to be the temple of the Lord and transformed it as the grave for our sins. God loves us so much, He was giving us plenty of times to live and journey into this world that one day we will call on God and knock on His heart to forgive us. But we humans are blindfolded by our pride and ego. This is the reason why Gods hates pride because with this we will lose our title to be called as the child of God and inherit of eternal life. Even we journey our present life in this earth our soul is been trapped by the death of pain and suffering. It is hard to find the real peace, joy and happiness that makes as content, satisfied and not to worry. Pure love and eternal peace are hidden and difficult to find. God said He is close to the broken-hearted. He said if you will seek me with all your heart you will find me. But in this troubled world which is Satan is the ruler, he will confuse the mind of the people to blame God for everything. As we all know that all people had given only a limited time to journey in this world and our soul will turn to where it belongs. We are being boastful to blame God when things go wrong for what we desire and also when our love ones departed this world. As it says in (1 John 2:15) Do not love the world or anything in the world. If anyone loves the world, the love of the Father is not in him. In (Ecclesiastes 12:7) it is said, and the dust will return to the earth as it was, and the Spirit will return to God who gave it.

We should learn to accept that everything we have does not belong to anyone even ourselves does not belong to us. Our body belongs to the earth and our soul belongs to God. This will prove that Heaven and earth will pass away but Gods word will remain. Once we depart in this world our times is ended and our love ones who are been left behind will continue their journey as a co-creator with God. And the only things we can give to them behind Is our memories, how did we act as a loving child of God and neighbours to others. Every human being is considered as a child of God by our equally same image of God through us which is our soul and we will distinguish by that as the child of God and not by colours, nationality, religion or any title that we carrying on in this world. We are not formed to be called a child of God by what we can see but with the power of Spirit which is unseen. God is a Spirit therefore we should journey ourselves by truth and Spirit so that we may live with His presence. We can love God and His bountiful of blessings from His love will be added unto us.

Psalm 139: 17-18

My thoughts towards you are countless as the sand on the seashore.

Every child that is born in this world was formed by love or by lust. But even a child is created by mistake of their earthly parents does it mean this child is a mistaken for God. Every innocent soul that is formed in the womb is out of sins. This child did not choose to come into this world with their choices it will come automatically by the nature of the works that their parents committed. They are not to blame, for others if a child was born because a man or a woman committed adultery they have already committed sins. It is wrong because every infant or child has an innocent soul because they did not put their heart to commit sins yet therefore their heart is pure and has an innocent soul for God. In this world some people who are not lawfully married to each other especially when they commit adultery because of lust if a child was born the crowd will recognized that his child is illegitimate. But for God, it is written in (Matthew 19:14) Jesus said, "Let the little children come to me, and do not hinder them, for the kingdom of heaven belongs to such as these."

Every little child has a pure and innocent soul they are free from sins this is the reason why Jesus gave the little children as an example to others.

It is written in (Matthew 18:3) then Jesus said, "I tell you the truth unless you turn from your sins and become like little children, you will never get into the kingdom of heaven." This is the reason why Jesus is calling everyone's heart to repent and sins no more because the wages of sins is death for your Spirit, and your soul which belongs to the realm of Spirit is not free from death the only way to see the kingdom of heaven is to submit your heart, mind and soul with all your strengths not to harm your soul from sins. Repentance is cleaning of mind, heart and soul out from the transgressions of sins that you committed at, and this will be and can be done only while we still exist in this world for once the Spirit of God who is living into our body was gone there is no turning back and it is too late. Our soul will face the consequences according to our deeds. In God we are all legitimate child, no soul is formed by other God. The only desire of the heart of God is we should walk and live all the time by His presence on walking in truth and Spirit until he comes back to take away the breath that He bestowed upon us. Each soul has given the time and limits to journey in this world. Not because a spirit is not formed yet properly as a human doesn't mean there is no life in there. When two eggs are joined together and formed blood inside the womb there is the Spirit of the Lord in there until it grows and formed as a human figure. The Spirit of the Lord must not be wasted by being abuse because of earthly desire and earthly explanation. We must take good care to our soul and the soul of others by walking obediently to God Free your soul from sins, reject the sins and live your life full towards godliness. This is the only way we can return to love God.

Zephaniah 3:17

And I rejoice over you with singing.

Every child that formed by love is a grace and gift for a family. Every member, relative and friends are joyful to see the coming of a new precious gift from God. Happiness and joy is a celebration for your love ones that you come into this world. They are all grateful to see you, to touch you and cuddled you. The parent must full of grace to be felt in love and formed a family with love. How are parents to be thankful and grateful for a coming of a child which is a gift from God is grace also for God that one of His innocent children was born and accepted to travel in this world? Each person must walk in purpose to love and be love. God put in His heart a parent to be called as an earthly angel that will look after their child and will teach them to walk in morality. In (Proverbs 22:6) It is said, train up a child in the way he should go, and when he is old he will not depart from it. In (Ephesians 6:4) Fathers, do not provoke your children to anger; instead, bring them up in the disciple and instruction of the Lord. As the role of a parent must teach their child to walk in truth, love, respect, kindness, generosity to build patience and understanding to walk in hand by being caring to one another. In (Deuteronomy 4:9) "Only give heed to yourself and keep your soul diligently, so that you do not forget the things which your eyes have seen and they do not depart from your heart all the days of your life, but make them known to your sons and your grandsons." As our duty as a parent and grandparents to our young ones is to show kindness to one soul and another to be righteous with all our ways to walk with great dignity by being honest and loyal to ourselves and another. This is the greatest form of perseverance to walk hand in hand in your family. And love, peace, joy and happiness will build oneself and another to be kind to their Spirit. As parents, we should walk in perseverance diligently as an example to our young ones so that when they grow old their heart and mind will walk to give favour to their soul to be out of sins and not harming their soul.

Jeremiah 32:40

I will never stop doing good to you.

As an earthly parent who put his/her love to their child. They are always kind and understanding to love and forgive their children. When their children made mistakes, yes parents get upset and try to correct their child not to do it again because what is done is wrong. Parents who love to walk in just and dignity even they are poor their hearts are formed to be good in honesty and loyalty. Therefore, correcting your children when they are a toddler or little child is much easier rather than when they grow as at the right age. Adolescent people are more rebellious when you correct them at that age. They have their mind and opinion for such thing even they are still immature. It is difficult to correct once a person's ego is uphand into their minds and heart. Every person has own character and behaviour, I didn't mean all grown-up people are perfect it depends on how they been trained and been disciplined when they were young. In (Jeremiah 29:11) It is said, "For I know the plans I have for you, declares the Lord," plans to prosper you and not to harm you, plans to give you hope and a future. In this troubled world which is Satan is the ruler. When trouble comes because we run out of self-control we are getting rebellious like as a beast. We don't have the patience to pause ourselves and questioning our mind why these things happenings to me. What was wrong that I should know so that I may correct it with silence and humbleness of heart to partake myself in repentance. Satan is very good on deceiving people. Some good people are always teased by the bad ones to get angry. No wonder the world is full of violence. Good people fight for justice but more people who turn evil to someone is creating more issue to be added so that the fierce of angriness, bitterness and resentment are enlarged in all human hearts. Forgiveness is a choice that we should submit our mind, heart and soul so that we may gain the blessings of the Lord through our life. Our future must be secured by having the wisdom and knowledge to respect and love our very own soul with perseverance towards to humbleness. For we are only travellers in this world, therefore, we don't have a future in here, means in this world. Our future must be on after our death in this world and it depends on how we create our journey when we still travelling in the world. Our future must be faced with consequences according to our deeds. It's either we go in heaven or in hell that is the last destination that our future will hold on to.

Exodus 19:5

For you are my treasured possession.

Every soul is very precious to God because these are all considered as His child and came out from His image. This is the reason why He sent Jesus His only begotten son to this world so that through Jesus we will find the kingdom of God and revealed unto us. In Jesus, through Jesus and by Jesus, we have complete and unrestricted access to the Father. We need not ever feel missing anything if we have asked Jesus to come in our lives. When we received the son we received the Father. In (John 14:23) Jesus said, "Anyone who loves me will obey my teaching. My Father will love them, and we will come to them and make our home with them." Therefore, if Jesus lives in us, then the Father lives in us and He has given us His Holy Spirit as a deposit of our guaranteeing our inheritance of eternal life. What a joy it is to be in a relationship with all the three persons in the Holy Trinity.

Jeremiah 32:41

I desire to establish you with all my heart and soul.

Do not be afraid to seek on God. His word is pure and full of righteousness. He will establish His covenant into your heart and mind so that through His words we were able to gain wisdom and understanding what is the true and real personality of our loving Almighty Father. When we received the gift of Jesus, the personality of the Father in heaven is also revealed and given to us. We will humble ourselves that we are only come from dust and will return to dust. Our soul is given and bestowed only to us and that does not belong to us for this is belong to God. We are not bound into something that we can say that is mine. Like the wind, we are transparent and living by senses and feelings. We didn't pay anything to be ourselves, it is completely free will be given to us. Therefore nothing belongs to us, we have given only the time and chances to journey in this world and one day will go to depart that is the nature of our life and circle of life. We are immune to this invisible power, no one man can ever have the power to refuse on that.

Jeremiah 33:3

And I want to show you great and marvellous things.

God chooses us to boil and sprout in this world so that we may be able to see the wonders of His works. He created this world as our home to live while we journey in this world. All the things are given to us before we are conceived in the womb. Parents are called to a possession as our protector and angel that who will take good care on us as our earth angel while we journey. They should be our first teacher in life who will teach us to walk in faith, love and hope through the valley of dignity and morality. But because of the lack of knowledge, we are easily broken and deceived. We losses are value and worth because we are not aware of what we are doing. We are always in to tap what makes pleases to the flesh and not to our Spirit. Most human believes that money is the source of everything. No wonder the world is living in the hell of confusion and death. People are not satisfied with what they have they forgot to live peacefully and joyfully because of chasing money. Money is evil and if you will attach to it your life which is supposedly limited will be stressed out and putting more troubles not to live normally and peacefully because of this. One day you will grow old and depart that you will feel and have the senses that you will never live. Even you have all your money and richness in this world you will not find comfort and peace. Sometimes on your last breath, you will see and find out that your family and relatives are only in for your richness. They will have a range of arguments because of the money that you will leave behind. All the things and money you gain even you say on your will that it will be buried in your grave it won't make it to happen because it is not useful for you anymore. The only things you can bring with is nothing else aside but your soul because once your life has passed away in this world it is formed to face on the judgement. If you keep only greediness, boastfulness, foolishness, angriness, bitterness and resentment you covered your life with pain and suffering and that is your reward and necklace of your soul. In (Matthew 6:20-21) It says, "But store up for yourselves treasures in heaven, where moths and vermin do not destroy, and where thieves do not break in and steal. For where your treasure is, there your heart will be also. God gave us the free will to live to love and felt love nothing else our journey is formed and bind with this to God and our neighbours. Don't let the richness of this world trap your soul in torment with pain, crying and sufferings."

Deuteronomy 4:29

If you will seek me with all thine heart, you will find me.

Adversity is a test and troubles in our life that will put ourselves to the test and challenges. God is very close to the broken-hearted. He is waiting for us to seek Him in great troubles and challenges of our life. He is powerful and He can surpass all our troubles if we will choose to surrender our heart in Him. God will help us to understand everything He is our greatest comforter in times of troubles when we learn to lean on Him and not on our understanding. God will give us knowledge and wisdom. If we feel rejected God will give us so many possibilities and dimensions to know and find our worth.

In (1 John 2:15) it is said, "Do not love the world or the things in the world. If anyone loves the world, the love of the Father is not in him. It is simply saying that the richness of the world belongs to Satan who is the ruler and the deceiver in this world."

Your soul which is considered the distinction to be called as the child of the Highest will be trapped in sins and this will cause death to your soul once you departed, your soul will face of consequences according to the decisions and actions that you have made when you are still in the world. God is the Father of all souls and this is the reason why God sent Jesus to this world to be the light for every soul so that anyone who will believe in Him and love Him their soul will be saved. Jesus is the greatest example to follow to keep away our soul in wrath. Journeying with the presence of the Lord by His words in every day of your life will give you grace, peace and comfort. Jesus conquers the grave and you as well when you learn to walk and live by the Spirit. You will not be deceived by the tactics of Satan to put your soul in pain and suffering. Satan has no power to mess up your life again. When someone will throw stones on you or stabbing in your back you will understand that they are blind, they do not know what they are doing. One eternal or,

Psalm 37:4

Delight in me and I will give the desires of your heart.

In this troubled world, every person wants to have a peaceful, joyful and contented life but finding this kind of happiness is not easy to find. In (Matthew 6:33) it is said, "But seek first the kingdom of God and this will be added unto you."

When we learn to understand what is in the mind and the desire of the heart of Jesus that is the moment we can have access to understand what is in the mind and the heart of the Lord. We can have the faith to live courageously and fearlessly for we know that we have given only a limited time to travel in this world. The source of everything comes to the Lord our God we are living by Spirit and not by the flesh alone. We know that it is our soul who is giving life for us to travel in this world. We will put our soul as our priority to love and care because the kingdom of God is not formed by material things or something that we can see by sight it is magically formed by Spirit. We will find to know that God is everywhere because His kingdom and personality is universal. We are all gathered and attached to one another by the power of His Spirit. Every living creature that moving and not moving is made from His Spirit therefore we are always living by with the presence of the Lord. It is true that no one can come to the Father without the presence of Jesus. In Jesus, with Jesus and by Jesus the kingdom of God will be revealed to us. Jesus is the exact representation of the personality of God. His knowledge and wisdom are not formed by the things we can see but it is formed by the invisible and magical power of Spirit. Therefore, a person who is born again by the gift of Jesus, he/she is not living anymore what makes pleases to the flesh for they understood that body is from dust and this will return to dust but their soul which is the source of their life will come back to where it belongs to once they are been departed to this world but before you get back on to where it belongs this will face first the judgement according to our deeds. How did we act and live while we still living on this planet? This is the reason Jesus did not come to abolish the Law of Moses but to be fulfilled it according to the grace and power of the law of one triune God which is the Holy Trinity. As you can see the God of Moses has put and added more law in the Ten Commandments which will confuse the mind and heart of people not to walk obediently to God for they will walk in the valley of death and suffering. Moses God promises is formed by ignorance not to know and give value to worth the life but to destroy it. Moses God is rebellious, dominant and not giving mercy to forgive but rather it will ignite the people to fight and create more battles to end the life. Satan's tactics are to finish and end life but because God is more powerful than him. He can put only suffering and death to other souls but because God knows that soul is formed to be evil because they are lack of knowledge and their choices are to follow Satan they are been condemned by their works not to inherit the eternal life. The power of the Lord is infinite this is the reason why it is said in the Gospel of the book of Matthew 24:35. Heaven and earth will pass away, but my words will never pass away. God is talking about the nature of the life of a person. Once a person dies they only have gone but the other gift from God that is been created with this person will get more to multiply. Each person has given only the times and opportunity to journey in this world temporarily so that we may see the marvellous creation and love of works of God. Each person has a purpose to walk and live by the love of the Spirit. Therefore walking and living by the Spirit is the greatest foundation of faith that we are from God and we belong to His kingdom and not in this world.

Philippians 2:13

For it is I who gave those desires.

Everyone has the desire to live eternally. People are afraid of death. But as we all can see the reality of life. We are only travellers in this world and we cannot have the power to refuse on that because our life does not belong to us. Our purpose here is to journey with love and to love one another. God is love and merciful and we should walk with this character towards one another. But because of Satan, the plan of God for all his children has changed. Human is being carried away to themselves to love the richness of this world and not to live normally and peacefully according to the presence of God. Humans even though they will depart they don't have really understand that after death every person will face the consequences base on each deed. So if your heart and mind are formed to be evil and boastful to your neighbours, your life must be full of hatred, bitterness, anger and resentment, you will never be happy and satisfied for your life. This is because you have broken soul, your evil actions and works to condemn towards to others have paid you in full of great pain, crying and suffering. You will never be happy, peaceful and content for the rest of your life if you haven't changed your heart and actions. The more rebellious you are the more you will find suffering. The only way to find out peace is to repent and forgive yourself for all the wrong-doings you have made. When you make peace to yourself it is easy for you to make peace to others. Sometimes people recognise your actions even you did not ask for forgiveness to the people you been hurt. God will make a marvellous sign for you that you are already forgiven. Some people that you hurt cannot fully turn back their trust to you but the most important is at least you will find that you are accepted and forgiven. These people can stand in front of you and they will not flee from you. Their heart is always kind to help you when you needed to. You can see that maybe they are away from you but you have to accept that things broken are not the same as it was. Always remember to give love and share the peace to your neighbours and God will bless you with abundant love physically, emotionally and spiritually you are healed, happy and content.

Free your soul from the power of your pride for this will destroy you.

Ephesians 3:20

I am able to do more for you than you could possibly imagine.

In (Matthew 6:33) it is said, "But seek first the kingdom of God and His righteousness, and all these things will be added unto you." God is a loving merciful God. His love is unconditional. He always gives us the favour to live freely with our choices. Sometimes and most of the times people always forgot to thank God for all the blessings that they have received from His hands. Honestly, people recognise only to call on God when they have problems but some people who are atheist don't believe in God. When trouble comes they don't kneel down and submit their heart to pray for God and ask to give them wisdom so that they may perform to deal with their problems with the presence of God. People are boastful because of their pride; some people will end to kill their lives. Some are weak and relying on others to deal with their problems and in the end, it will break them completely. God said if you will look for me wholeheartedly, you will find me. Having the wisdom from God is a beginning of knowledge. God will help you to visualise your problems and will give you guidance on how to deal with your problems fearlessly. Your faith will be unshakable, your strength has come from God no one has the power to be-little you. You will stand firm; no one can ever break you for your heart will be trained diligently with prudence. The blessings of the Lord which come from the Holy Spirit will come upon you always as a shield for your life.

2 Thessalonians 2:16-17

For I am your greater encourager.

In every adversity or troubles in our life, God is always with us. Our body is his temple that is why He is familiar in all our ways. God is our greater encourager if we choose to submit our heart on Him. He will guide us in every aspect of our lives. He is our greatest comforter in all troubles that will help us to build ourselves as a Spirit warrior for God. In this world, the battle is Spirit to Spirit. Positive and negative people always have conflicts with each other. Positive people always work in demand for morality but negative one always leads on to confusion that will give favour always to their ego. Positive peoples believe in truth and always have the heart to walk in a moral way of dignity, integrity and humility. They always love their works injustices by love, hope and trust with great perseverance towards righteousness and loyalty. Negative people instead works in great complain, they are self-centred, egoistic and they always believe in lies even you simply showed mercy to believe in facts of truth. Negative people don't show mercy and compassion to the Spirit who is living within them these are the reason why they are not easy to mingle on. They were living in expectations, they are selfish, dictator and manipulators who always condemn and blame others when things won't get to what pleases them. When you are in a relationship with this kind of person like as a spoiled brat you will always have troubles and conflict. They are the bossy type and you should always listen to them. They will lead your neck like a dog. And if you allow them to ruled your choices for your life, they will be happy to make it for you. They won't allow you to stand as you are into yourself and that makes you feel unhappy to yourself. As a person who is given only limited times to journey in this world because we are only travellers, you should take in your hands to stand yourself as who you really are. Respect yourself first and don't allow others to treat you in disgrace. Keep yourself positive and always lean on God and not on your understanding and you will always have peace in your mind and heart no matter what. Spread your wings for you are ready to fly like as an eagle. The happy and contented person knows their capacity and their worth and they are not relying on others. They believe within themselves that they can do it.

2 Corinthians 1:3-4

I am also your Father who comforts you in all your troubles.

God did not give as a timid Spirit. Inside of us, we are all warriors of God which is always young and useful. Our purpose in this world is known for being merciful to our soul and the soul of others. Always remember that if God is for us no one will be against us for it is God who will give us the strength to fight our battles on our knees. He will give us the prudence of our works to believe that everything happens for a reason and should take the possibility to find out that reason. And once you find out that reason you will take that challenges and adversities is a gift for you to find out your worth. And when you find out your worth struggles, challenges and adversity are only fleas that need to be defeated. Face your fear and your fear will flee from you. For this has no power to destruct and ruined you. And in your heart, you will mark to believe that as long as God is giving me life to live a fighter will never give up.

Psalm 34:18

When you are broken-hearted, I am close to you.

When adversities tap in your life and your faith in God is not completely build up yet. Adversity will challenge your life to be worried and full yourself of anxiety. Sometimes at the very end, you will question God why is it all this suffering is coming on to you. Even deep on your heart you know that you are kind and loving to others. You will question yourself Why these people you love and you gave up everything for them will treat you in a nasty way. In (Mark 6:4) Jesus said to them, "A prophet is not without honour except in his town, among his relatives and in his home." Honestly, we are always put to the test to the people who are very close to us. We ended up in suffering when we treat our love ones as our greater priority. These people sometimes won't consider your feelings, as long as they needed you and you will help them to supply for their needs you will feel you're so important to them because it will please them. But as long as they will feel that you are not useful for them anymore. Every decision that you will make for your life is not good for them. They are afraid that you will leave them behind and they are not important for you anymore. It is always happening in the family. This is the reason why some families will end up broken. They don't allow their love ones to journey their life in their way. They are so attached that a human that who is belong to them will always to give favour to please them and not others or even to their very own selves. Brokenness always comes to the people who were you are close to. But once you seek on God by asking why this all suffering comes to you for all the goodness you have done for others. God will teach you another perspective in your life that no one in this earth can ever give you. God will form yourself as a new creation without living your life in expectations. You will work to start to love yourself for not being aware of everything. He will give you a new heart and new understanding that will lead yourself to lean on God and not on human understanding. You will understand that you do not belong to this world because you belong to Him. You have just given only limited times to journey in this world by with His presence. And from then you will love your soul by repenting from your sins and forgive others for they do not know what they are doing. You will be called in purpose to love God and love your neighbours as yourself. Two great commandments of Jesus are revealed on to you. And that is the greatest blessings that you can ever have and received. Satan has no more power to hurt and kill your soul for God has helped you to find your way back to Him. Peace, happiness, joy and contentment are your grace until the end. No more pain, crying and suffering for God has healed you. You will find that the source and confusion of everything came from your pride. And God will help you to let go of your pride and let the love of God be the centre of your life.

Isaiah 40:11

"As a shepherd carries a lamb, I have carried you close to my heart."

Our breath of life comes from the same image of God. This is the one magnificent source of that we are conformed by the same Spirit of God. Every soul is lambs of God, this is our identity that we are belongs to God. For a man without Spirit in his body will be dead. God wants us all to give favour to the Spirit that is been given and bestowed to us to walk and live by truth and Spirit while we journey until we finish our days to live in this planet. God stands by us by keeping our body as His temple. Once God rips this Spirit away from our body, we don't have a purpose at all to co-create and make ourselves useful. For once our time has ended to live on this planet our body will turn back to dust for this was came from dust. It is an opportunity for us to be a co-creator for God to share love and respect not only to humans but also to all the richness of Mother Earth. Our world is our home while we travel in this world and we should keep it divine and useful for everyone. But because humans love and greediness for the sake of money, title, fame, popularity, etc. dooms the world by discriminations towards one another. People act like beasts, they reject others soul to live on this planet. They use their money to think that they are ahead and better than anyone else and yet the truth is even you have the richness of this world your life will be cast away from this world too. No one man can ever escape and say that they can live on this planet eternally. The world is been broken because of having the mind like these. Humans should know by heart that everyone is the same in the eyes of the Lord. He hasn't had favourites, that will last themselves to live on this planet even the prophets and disciples are gone. God carries our souls by the grace of His heart and mind to be one and have eternal communion with Him. But because of sins, human's heart is being separated to God. They love things and rejected their very own soul for the sake of money. People are being slaved by money and all the richness of this world. Jesus the only begotten Son of God came to be the light in this world so that anyone who will believe in Him will not be slave of the power of money. They will not worry about what they will eat or what they will use to wear for in the deepest part of their heart, they know and have the desire that God will provide as long as we are not lazy. God will help ourselves to work for our needs so that we may have the blessings from His hand. God is a good and loving Father that will teach his child to move forward in morality that will give grace not only to our flesh but most to our Spirit. Keep your body alive and divine for Godly purposes and God will give and bring us a nice banquet for ourselves to journey in this world peacefully, joyfully and content.

Revelation 21:3-4

One day I will wipe away every tear from your eyes.

And I'll take away all the pain you have suffered on this earth.

Once we tap to gain and know God's personality, we submit ourselves to lean on God and not on our own understanding. For it is true that the love of the Lord works in mysterious ways. These are the reason why God said my thoughts are not your thoughts. Once you understand what is in the mind and the heart of Jesus, you are capable to do the impossible things. You will put in your heart the desire to create your dreams. Like for example, you know that in your actual life and deep in your heart you don't have knowledge about to do something because the crowds will hurt and criticised you because of the standards of your life but if God will call you to do something if you will follow that desire it will come to pass and blessings to your life because you are capable to share your genius work to others. We are called to share wisdom and knowledge to others and our purpose in the community and society is the adherence to live out from ignorance but has a purpose to be the light and salt into others' lives. God wants us all to find our worth to journey with courage and put our trust on Him. And He will shape us to believe that nothing is impossible if you will believe you can do it. We should need to come out from our shell as long as God is allowing us to live. We have a purpose to find our way back home. Yes, we were put to the test by fires of troubles and heartaches but the scars that left will remind us to awaken our Spirit that we do not belong to this earth but in the presence of the Lord. Heaven is here now when you learn to walk by faith with the truth and personality of the Spirit. God is a Spirit and our souls belong to the Kingdom of the Spirit. Our flesh is from dust and this will return to dust. Now once you learn that, you will not be afraid anymore to travel in this world for you know deep in your heart that the love of the Lord to your soul has saved you to live peacefully and joyfully. You will accept that one day you will depart in this world because God has ended your times to travel. We should humble ourselves to accept the truth that we have given only limited times to journey with the presence of the Lord so do not be deceived by the richness of this world. This is the reason why it is said in (1 John 2:15) "Do not love the world or the things in the world."

If anyone loves the world, the love of the Father is not on him. Remember the owner of the richness of the world is Satan, who will be deceived and put the hearts and minds of all in the confusion that will lead every soul in the torment of pain, crying and suffering. This is the reason why when Satan offered the richness of the world to Jesus because Jesus has the mind and heart of the Father in heaven. He knows that Satan's purpose is to deceive one soul and another to end up by suffering Jesus rejected the offer of Satan. Jesus should give up His body because He knows that deep in His heart that his flesh was from dust and this will return to dust because this belongs to the earth and not to God. His soul belongs to God and our souls belong to God as well that is why we should love and care to our Spirit as our priority. Love your soul and you will be free from pain, crying and suffering. God will bless you with the new life that you will choose to give merit to your soul than to your flesh. Your earthly desires will come to an end and you will start your life to walking obediently to God with His presence in every moment and every day of your life. From then the Holy Spirit is the one who will lead your life.

John 17:23

I am your Father and I love you even as I love my son, Jesus.

Jesus and all the people in this world are considered as one equal child by God through our souls. Jesus came to the world to be the light in this world for every soul. Every human being that will put their heart to believe in Jesus will have the gift of the Holy Spirit. The Holy Spirit who is living in our body will lead us to make decisions that will give us always to our soul to journey with the presence of God and what makes pleases to the Holy Spirit. In (Mark 3:28-30) it is said, "Truly, I say to you, all sins will be forgiven the children of man, and whatever blasphemies they utter, but whoever blasphemes against the Holy Spirit never has forgiveness, but is guilty of an eternal sin—" for they were saying, "He has an unclean spirit."

Every human being was been blindfolded about the truth. The mark of the beast is been implanted to our hearts this is the reason why we are easily deceived to angriness, bitterness, resentment, insecurities, anxiety and so on. We haven't understood that our true if blood from God is our soul and not the blood that flows from our veins. Some people have thought that the blood that is flowing in our body is sacred and we should forbid ourselves not to eat it with flesh.

In (Mark7: 18-20) it is said, "Are you so dull?" He asked. "Don't you see that nothing that enters a person from the outside can defile them? For it doesn't go into their heart but into their stomach, and then out of the body." (In saying this, Jesus declared all foods clean.) He went on: "What comes out of a person defiles them." Certainly, when we criticised people with angriness, bitterness and resentment in our heart without giving the knowledge of the facts of truth, we are being defiled because we are speaking by falsehood to our neighbours. And this is a blasphemy to the Holy Spirit which is unforgivable sins. Adultery is a blasphemy also towards the Holy Spirit. Pride and lust are favour to Satan and with this Satan will govern each person to deceived and have an unclean Spirit. People are being boastful because of their pride. Their heart and mind will have a carrying unforgiving spirit and this will condemn their soul in pain and suffering. Cheating and lies will also condemn your soul.

In pain and suffering and will cause you a broken relationship. Our body is the temple of the Holy Spirit therefore when we are being rebellious and liars to others. We put ourselves in being rebellious to God first and not into our neighbour. This is the reason why Jesus said to repent and sins no more. And when our times have ended our soul will be free and have the title of being called as the child of God again, eternal life are our rewards for the future after that our soul is been judge according to our deeds after our death here on earth.

John 17:26

For in Jesus, my love for you is revealed.

Jesus is sent by God as the light of the world. "The true Messiah in this troubled world and only begotten son of the Lord, He came to this world as the greatest example to follow that will teach people to walk in truth and by Spirit. Through Jesus, we can have access to see the kingdom of God. The thought of Jesus is from the garden of wisdom and knowledge of the Lord. His word is the lamp to our feet and the light into our path. The grace and love of the Lord towards us is revealed on to Him. Jesus is the chosen one that will help other people to love their soul to walk in righteousness. He did not come to abolish the law but to fulfil the law. In (John 1:17) It is said, for the law was given to Moses, but God's unfailing love and faithfulness came through Jesus. The God of Noah and Abraham until Moses has formed of confusion. Hates ignite to ruin and wasted the Spirit at that time. Their God is dominant and has a heart of full of violence that will confuse the mind of people to create more troubles rather than to forgive and be merciful towards one another. Peace and grace to be loving and caring to one another from that time are still dead in the hearts of many. Egyptians and Jewish people have always conflict with each other. And these was been inherited from that time until now. Jesus was born to be the light in this world to bring peace, love and unity but because of the Law of Moses, most people are still blind and still not accepting Jesus into their hearts. Satan used Noah, Abraham and Moses as the greatest prophet of the world but these men don't know the Holy Spirit. Their hearts are blind about what is the truth that we human beings are only given the chance to live here on this planet temporarily. And we should rather live ourselves what makes please to the Spirit rather than to our flesh. When we receive the grace of gift from Jesus we received God. Knowledge and wisdom is opened also to us to know the truth. We will look also on the heart of works of the prophets who and which one they will follow. Confusions and troubles are not answered by the teachings of Noah, Abraham and Moses. Only through Jesus, the true personality of a loving and merciful God is been revealed. We should be baptised and born again by the Holy Spirit through Jesus Christ. This is the only way that we were able to love God and love our neighbours as ourselves. The truth will be revealed to us and will take our hearts to repent and sin no more, for we have gained the knowledge that our soul will be in torment because sins is a pandemic disease in this world that will kill your soul."

Hebrew 1:3

He is the exact representation of my being.

From the beginning, the world is void and has no life and only the Spirit of God hovered over the waters. Jesus has come to this world magically by the presence of the Spirit of the Lord. The Lord sent Archangel Gabriel to see and told to Mary who is a virgin woman that she will conceive a child by the grace of the Holy Spirit and this child will be called Jesus. Mary gets magically pregnant by the Holy Spirit and through the Holy Spirit Jesus was born. Jesus knowledge and wisdom come from the Holy Spirit, which is the Supernatural Father of all Spirit. God's presence is universal this is the reason why Jesus is talking his scriptures in parables. The personality of God is hard to understand by human understanding, without the grace of the Holy Spirit the thoughts and mind of Jesus are not easily captured to understand. The personality of God is given to Jesus and through Jesus, we were able to have communion with the heart of God. The kingdom of God will also reveal on to us through Jesus Christ. Jesus is the light, the truth and the way no one can come to the Father without Him. Believe in Jesus and we are called to be born again as a new creation and child of God. And we will transform ourselves what will gives favour to the Spirit of the Lord rather than to our flesh. We will find out that our time's here on earth is limited because our soul does not belong to this world but in the Kingdom of God.

Romans 8:31

He comes to demonstrate that I am for you, not against you.

Jesus is been sent by God to this world. So that through Him the kingdom of God will be revealed to us. His words and teachings are the stream of life and living water for every soul to live peacefully and joyfully with the presence of our loving Almighty Father. Jesus is full of knowledge and wisdom from the Holy Spirit. His grace is sufficient from all matters. Jesus thought is from God and not from human understanding. His heart is not formed by earthly desire but in a heavenly kingdom that will give us peace, happiness and comfort in everyday of our life. Jesus has come to this world to be the light and demonstrate the love of the Lord to us. He is the chosen one who will help us to lift up our soul to be out from the power of darkness of sins because the wages of sins is death for one soul and another. Our soul is from God and these belong to the Kingdom of God but when our soul is been contaminated by the mark of the beast the light of our soul will be diminished and no life at all. Pain and suffering are the rewards in every day of your life when you walk and live by what makes pleases to your flesh because of being rebellious to the Holy Spirit. Sins are the opposite of love, this is the reason why there are heaven and hell. Sins are the fruit of Satan that will put the mind, heart and soul of humanity in darkness of pain and suffering, the soul which is our lifeblood from God will be in great torment because of sins. And love is purely divine from the essence of the Lord because one of the personality and character of God is known by love: "God is love."

2 Corinthians 5:18-19

And to tell you that I am not counting your sins. Jesus died so that you and I could be reconciled.

Jesus thought to people that we should submit our mind to accept and understand that our body is the temple of the Lord. And God lives in us, every wrong-doings that will hurt the Spirit because of the choices that make pleasing to the flesh and the pride, reject the Spirit. And when we reject the Spirit who is living into the bodies of our neighbours we did blasphemy and slandered the Holy Spirit. It is said that the unforgivable sin is when we slandered the Holy Spirit. "God always has the heart to love and forgive us." He knows that all child is been contaminated by the mark of the beast which is pride. All of God's people are been lost because of a lack of knowledge about what are the truth and the true real personality of God. Humans are easily boastful to criticise one soul and one Spirit by their perverse speech, evil behaviour and arrogance because of the pride. Most people have a lack of self-control, they are not kind to other soul and their soul as well. This is the reason why the world is in great confusion because of pride. Pride is the source of pain and suffering in this world. In (Proverbs 8:13) Says, to Fear the Lord is to hate evil; I hate pride and arrogance, evil behaviour and perverse speech. God hates pride because it won't show love and respect to the Spirit. Pride will like to hurt and kill the soul in troubles of pain, crying and suffering. This is the reason when a person is being led by their pride or ego they talk out of righteousness to one being and another. They criticise people badly without knowing the facts and even a person is giving reason about the truth, prideful people won't really agree or accept that. People in this world are full of liars and hypocrite and dealing with them will not bring you peace. So when you know the truth and revealed it to anyone who has lack of knowledge and they keep believe in lies, it is so much better you shake off your feet and go rather than pushing them to believe in truth and just. Ignorant people don't believe in truth they believe in lies this is the reason they are living their life in a great complaint, expectations and most likely blaming others for their sufferings. They love gossiping others life to destroy others dignity makes them please their pride but the consequences are never ending troubles and heartaches to their soul. Pride is the mark of the beast that put the souls to be killed and destroyed. It is absolutely wrong to give favour to love pride because you will reject God to be the centre of your life. So if God is still giving you a day to live in this world, learn to know these matters and use your mind what will give honour in truth and Spirit rather than lies and flesh.

Jesus died in the cross even he has an innocent soul and out of sins, for the sake of many. God's love is fulfilled in the life of Jesus. Jesus is the greatest example to everyone that will put the heart of many to be more courageous and have no fear to whom has the power to kill the body but has no power to kill the soul. Jesus heart and actions of understanding will apprehend to anyone that we should recognise that we have given only limited times to journey in this world and we should understand to Love our soul and gives favour to love the souls of others for the lives of many depends on the Spirit and not on the flesh or the richness of this world. The richness of this world will drown our Spirit to death. And Satan is the ruler of this world the one who is in charge to put everyone's heart, mind and soul in condemnation of pain, crying and suffering. Jesus wants to inform everyone that the richness in this world will put our soul to be paid in death. Sins are from Satan and this will cast out all the souls out from heaven but be delivered to the fires of hell because the wages of sins is death for every soul. Jesus is encouraging us to repent and sin no more because the truth and the love of the Father which *is* in heaven are given to Him and will be revealed to us by believing on him. This is the reason why it is said in (1 John 2:15) "Do not love the world or anything in the world. If anyone loves the world, the love of the Father is not in him."

But look upon on the things that you can't see. For the unseen thing is eternal and the things you saw from your sight are only temporary. No one man can live by flesh alone for a body is from flesh and this belongs to the richness of this world because this is from the earth and the earth it will return. Our soul comes from the Spirit and this will return in the realm of the Spirit for these belong to the Spirit. The soul is the life which is invisible to see but have the grace to move our being into life. God is a Spirit where all life is come from supernaturally.

1 John 4:10

How to love our neighbours as ourselves? Through Jesus, we can go back to the Lord and our sins will be forgiven. Peace and happiness is our reward on this earth until we go back to the kingdom of God. No more pain, crying or suffering for God has pulled us out from the power of Satan who will put our soul to death.

Romans 8:31-32

I gave up everything I loved that I might gain your love.

God has given us all the privilege to journey each day with our free will and choices. Even so many times we didn't realise that when we commit sins we hurt His feelings, we are being beast that we treat His temple as the grave for our sins. And every time that we choose to gives favour to our flesh "We rejected Him as our Father." Our soul has diminished the light and the darkness of sins captured it into pain, crying and suffering. Sins put our soul in dangers of death. God is always merciful, loving and kind to us. His love is unconditional until to the last of our breath in this world. He gave us many chances to look and search for Him and ask for His forgiveness but because humans are blind and easy to deceive. Humans are not finding their ways to go back to our Almighty Father who is the Father of all souls. Humans love much the richness of the earth and when the day will come that God will come back to take the life that is given to anyone, humans are afraid to die. They are so attached to the world. They just have forgotten that we have given only the privilege and limited times to travel in this world and our true home is in the kingdom of God which is the one Jesus has talking to while he still journeying in this world. Our Almighty Father did all His best so that we may be able to give our lives back to Him through Jesus Christ. He sent Jesus into this world so that we may have access to go back ourselves in the presence of the Lord our Almighty Father. But even Jesus has paid in full the love of the Lord on to the cross. Humans did not get His knowledge and wisdom about in heavenly kingdom. Humans are still blind about our true nature of life does not come to this world but only from the grace of the Spirit. Satan is incharge to this world, he is the ruler of this world that will put every soul in condemnation by the power of darkness and death. He will mislead people to love their body that will make pleases to their flesh rather than to their Spirit who is living within them. Humans haven't dignified that the source of everything comes from the Spirit this is the reason why many are lost because of lack of knowledge.

1 John 2:23

If you receive the gift of my son Jesus, you receive me.

The gift of the Holy Spirit is soft as the flakes of the snow. It won't harm you but it will give you the grace of being kind to yourself not to harm your very own soul. He will give you wisdom and understanding that will soothe in your life to journey with gratitude in your heart. Peace and happiness will shine inside the core of your being. No one in this earth will able to brake or ruin your title as the child of God. For you will be a loss but then found by the grace of the Holy Spirit. In everyday of your life, you are going to be fruitful of love and the grace of the Lord will live in your life. You will be more aware not only to yourself but also to others. You will have the knowledge of understanding if a person is being marked by the beast, for their works will be showing it to you. Their hearts are boastful and unforgiving they always like to feed their pride and not their conscience. It is easier for them to harm their souls and others. When the Holy Spirit leads your life, you will walk with prudence to be more truthful, loving and grateful to the innocent child of God who is living within you. Your soul will be enlightened by the grace and power of love. God is love and our soul will be comforted by His love because our soul belongs to love and not in this world who is the ruler is Satan.

Romans 8:38-39

And nothing will ever separate you from my love again.

Once you are been baptised and receive the gift of Jesus. You are not the same person as before. Your mind is set upon on the kingdom of God. In every time that God has given you a day to travel in this world. You will walk by the presence of the love of the Holy Trinity. Your body will be their temple for their words is alive into your heart and gives you the strength to live fearlessly. You will have the idea to love always and makes your soul pure and clean out by the darkness of sins. You know that sin is a pandemic disease in this world that is not easily be cured without putting yourself into repentance. Only through repentance, you will have the knowledge to put your heart into convictions. Yes, you will understand that because you were blind about the truth and the grace of God before, you will certainly do what makes please to your flesh and your pride. But then Holy Spirit will give you the light of understanding to be more loving, joyous, peaceful, forbearance, kindness, goodness, faithfulness, gentleness and self-control to love your soul. This is the beginning of a new life for you. Your heart will not be formed anymore to earthly desire. You will not condemn anymore your soul to be hurt and live in pain, crying and suffering. For the truth and the grace of God has set you free. You will store up your treasure in heavens by being respectful and loving to the Holy Spirit that is living into your body and your neighbour's body. In (1 Corinthians 6:19} It is said, Do you not know that your bodies are the temple of the Holy Spirit, who is in you, whom you have received from God? You are not your own. In (Matthew 12:31-32) says, "And so I tell you, every sin and blasphemy will be forgiven men, but the blasphemy against the Spirit will not be forgiven." Anyone who speaks a word against the Son of Man will be forgiven, but anyone who speaks against the Holy Spirit will not be forgiven, either in this age or in the age to come. Therefore you will keep your body as pure and divine only for heavenly and Godly purposes. Satan will have no more power to hurt your soul and he will flee from you. You will journey your days with great confidence for God has strengthened you to love and be love. And the love of God for your soul endures forever. Eternal life is given to your soul to live on love and kindness.

Luke 15:7

Come home and I'll throw the biggest party Heaven has ever seen.

Every child of God is important to God. He sent Jesus to this world to be as an example to follow and be the light to other souls. With Jesus teachings, we were able to be baptised and born again as a new creation of God. Jesus mentioned many times to repent and sin no more for this is the only way we can be cleansed and purified again our soul. Seeking for God for His forgiveness for every transgression we have made is walking and putting our heart to humbly ourselves that we are only from dust and to dust will return. Jesus came to save the souls of many because they were contaminated by the mark of the beast. At an early age, humans have an innocent soul and child for God because they did not turn against yet to the Holy Spirit. All they can do is to show peacefulness, joyfulness and contentment that everything they need must be given to them freely by the love of their parents. God put the desire into their parents to love and care for their child with kindness and not expecting in return. Every smile that child gives to their parents is a sign of love and saying of thank you which the parent cannot have to resist to shares their love by hugs, cuddles and kisses. The desire of Jesus and our Almighty Father are one. Their purpose is to help people to renew their mind and change their heart to walking obediently what makes pleases to the Spirit than to our flesh. For our flesh belongs to the richness of this world. And one day it will go back and buried to the earth for the soul belongs to God. And this is why Jesus accepted himself to be put in the cross for the sake of many. We human beings are equally the same child by the same grace of Spirit of God. Anyone who will believe in Jesus will not perish for the Father, the Son and the Holy Spirit is fully alive in their heart, mind and soul. God wants us all His child (soul) will be saved and have the inheritance of eternal life after our death in this world. The joy of the Father and the son which is bound again to be united are precious for they will both feel accepted and loved by one another. Every sinner that is been lost will found their worth on believing on Jesus by receiving their title to be called their soul as a child of God again. Conviction is a wisdom that will guide our ways to go back to purified again our soul as to be like as an innocent child of God. Free from sins and your soul will be from death. Your soul will be saved by pleasing God and not to makes you please by earthly and lustfully desire.

Ephesians 3:14-15

I have always been Father and will always be Father.

Our Almighty Father is the source of everything. He is the Alpha and Omega. Our life has come from Him and when our purpose has ended to journey in this world. He will judge us according to our deeds on how did we care and love His Spirit while we still exist in the world? Did we really care to be with His presence or we rejected Him by our earthly choices. God looks upon into our hearts and He knows who would be his child or not in His sight. God looks upon the heart of humbleness towards truthfulness and righteousness. He knows who is the Her and the deceiver for He knows that their actions will give favour to their pride to turn evil to their neighbours (co-travellers in this world). The fruit of the fool will give favour to what their pride dictates them to do it.

They don't have self-control because they listen to their pride. This is the reason why they are being rebellious not only to God but also to others. They have forgotten that the key to the gates to heaven is Jesus. He is the one who will encourage people to walk, live and love the Spirit that is living within them. When we learn to walk and live by Spirit the grace of the Lord will come upon us and we will never be separated again by His presence. We were able to conquer the grave for our soul will live eternally by the power and presence of God. Our Almighty Father is always our Father in Spirit which is invisible to the eyes but when we learn to use our heart. We may be able to understand everything about on Spirit.

John 1:12-13

My question is…Will you be my child?

God's heart is waiting for us to know if our heart, mind and soul are formed only into His presence. Does our soul is really conformed into His kingdom? Every soul is the lifeblood for every child of God. Do we really know and understand that our soul came from the same image of God? Do we really understand and captured the message of God in Jesus teachings? Do we really believe and follow Jesus as our brother and saviours of each humankind soul'? What kind of participation we will do and must do that God our Almighty Father will be convinced to believe? Does our Faith is strong enough like as Jesus? It is true that our Almighty Father looks upon what is been kept in our heart and not on our physical appearance. How can we ever say we love God when our actions and deeds did not show love and mercy to be more compassionate to care and love the Spirit which is living within in our body? Jesus said that our body is the temple of the Lord. If in our actions we transformed our body as the grave for our sins, have we had the knowledge that we hurt God's child (soul) into suffering because the wages of sins is death for the each and everyone's soul? Jesus was calling everyone's heart to repent and sin no more. In your life have you ever check your conscience and being honest to yourself that you did not take actions of blasphemy against the Holy Spirit. God wants us all to be out of sins and followers of Jesus to bring back the light and peace again into this world. Our heart should be like as Jesus who will help others to enlightening also other souls to be out of death (sins). This is the only way we can be called His child again. Repent and sin no more so that we may gain the reward of eternal life after our death into this world which is being considered. The first heaven for this world is been created as a paradise for every child of God. The second heaven is when the personality of God is been revealed to us and help us to change our mind and heart not to harm our soul because He found that *our* soul is the key for eternal life. The third heaven is after we finish our Journey to travel in this world and we have the knowledge and understanding that our soul will be saved and out from death. We will go and leave this planet peacefully and joyfully for we are ready to meet our eternal Father, who is the source of everything called life.

Luke 15:11-32

I am waiting for you.

When Jesus has finished to accomplishing the purpose that is given to him by our invisible and Almighty Father to share the love of God to others. In the heart of our Almighty Father, he is longing that every soul that is considered to His child will turn back to Him and never be lost again. In every day of our life, we should learn to turn ourselves into a conviction to give praises and love the Spirit for this is the true nature of the kingdom of God. When we praise God by not seeking earthly desire has to offer for us. The doors of heaven will be open to us. God will give us the desire in our heart to manifest this desire by being creative and motivating ourselves to make it happen. It is like dreams come true by putting ourselves into hard working. So do I in our Faith, to believe in Jesus is the first step but accepting Jesus in our lives is another stage of learning. And living with the presence of Jesus in everyday of our life is a complete work of our faith in God. Following Jesus and spreading the Gospel is not easy but it is worthy. Yes, you will be condemned by many. You will be criticised, hated and persecuted. Some will say you are insane and out of your mind but for you when you received the wisdom and knowledge of Jesus through your experience it will not bother you because deep in your heart. You will understand that these people did not come yet to the point to see what you have seen and understand what you have understood. These people are blindfolded by their ego and pride. This is the reason why Jesus said if His kingdom is here on earth His people will fight for him to be protected but the kingdom of Jesus is not easily revealed on the eyes but it is completely understood by the very deep part of our heart which is not easily understood by human understanding. The Holy Spirit is the one who will give you His fruit to understand everything. Jesus was been sent to this world by our Almighty Father to be an example and light to others. God is waiting for us to walk like as Jesus as the light also to this world for the souls of many. Our Almighty Father was calling in our hearts into convictions to live and journey our days which will give favour to love the Spirit and the Spirit that is living into our neighbours. As we all know that we are only travellers in this world. Every human being that lives in this world is our neighbours. Parents, brothers, sisters, spouse and every member of our family is our first neighbour in this world that we will journey with us. And we should give love and respect to the Spirit that lives not only into our body but to them also. Then multiply to others even if we knew them or not. Respect, love and unity must be gained and applied first in the family then to society and the whole world. Be the light and salt to others. When there is a rain of troubles and confusion in the gathering of family. Forgiveness is not easy to be given especially if it is your love ones who caused you pain and suffering. Unless you were being baptised by the grace of the Holy Spirit. You will be able to let go of unforgiving Spirit towards them. You will set yourself to untie by being angry and full of resentments because of your pride. Holy Spirit will uphold you to know your worth through Jesus Christ. You will forgive yourself by being ignorant and allowing the pride to ruin your life. You will have the wisdom and understanding why these people who are angry and hates you acted you in that way because the truth is. It is the pride who governs their life to live in that behaviour. Even they did not seek for you to forgive them. Your heart is wide open to forgive them by letting them go of their rebellious actions towards you. You know that when they spit bad words to you they are the one who is hurting themselves and not you. They don't have peace, joy and contentment in their life. The fruit of the Holy Spirit will lead your life into silence and waiting for the time to them to realise that they are wrong in their grievous actions. And that is what happened to all the high priest who put Jesus on the cross. After Jesus died on the cross they realise that Jesus is the true Messiah and Son of God. We are only travellers in this world and God will come back to us in unexpected times. Proving that no one is the best or better than anyone else. The question is are we ready? When those times will come. The only legacy that we can leave into this planet is our memories of Faith, love, peace, hope and joy for this is eternal. And it is not kept only into our mind but most into our heart.

Matthew 6:19-21

Do not store up for yourselves treasures on earth, where moth and vermin destroy, and where thieves break in and steal. But store up for yourselves treasures in heaven, where moths and vermin do not destroy, and where thieves do not break in and steal. For where your treasure is, there your heart will be also.

Humility, integrity and morality are our greatest treasures that we should keep in our hearts. Charity is an act of love with great dignity that we give compassion to love our soul and the souls of others and in response to love the universe by respecting the Holy Spirit. This is the divine love of creating and motivating one person and another to have the heart of prudence by walking in love, mercy and compassion by standing in truth and journeying their soul or our souls by the grace and love of the Holy Trinity.

The riches of this world cannot help us to save our souls but will put our souls into condemnations of being trapped in the death of our souls. People who put their heart to love the riches of this world are selfish, self-centred and egoistic. And most don't really believe in God. They believe in the power of their money and sometimes they treat people as slaves. They treat people as not equal to them and as fellow travellers. They think they are better than anyone else. This is what we see in the parables of Lazarus and the rich man. The rich man did not give mercy to love and considerate the soul of Lazarus. He has in mind and his heart that human being is like an animal that should not be treated by love and mercy. It is said that after our death here on earth our soul will be put to judgement according to our deeds and faith that we have put in God.

So, if God is giving you the time to go back with Him as the Father of all after you have known the truth. Would you care to start and love your soul to be out of death by journeying your days by the presence of the Holy Spirit? The choice is yours to repent and sin no more.

Part-Three
The Picture of the World

Genesis 1:1-2

When God began to create the heavens and the earth, the earth had no form and was void; darkness was over the deep and the Spirit of God hovered over the waters.

By the seventh day the work of God was completed, and He rested on the seventh day. God put the Man to be in charge to look after the world as the paradise to live. But the fall came when the woman that was given to Adam was deceived by Satan to eat the fruit of the tree of knowledge between good and evil which was forbidden to them not to eat. Satan has then had access to interfere with the life of a child of God. The world was doomed by the power of darkness of Satan. Humans stand as boastful because of the fruit that is been eaten is contaminated by the beast. These are the reasons why people lost their lives to inherit eternal life. The lightness that they have for their life was being virus by darkness. These are the reason why the hearts of all humanity are formed like this tree of knowledge between good and evil. We have the part of being good to do good works but when our heart is being troubled by our pride. We don't have the self-control to pause ourselves to re-channel our mind to see if we're going to do is evil or not. Inside of us we have two wolves which have always fighting which one will you give favour wins. When you give favour for your conscience you will walk in humbleness to live and walk by the truth that will please to God. But when pride is in charge, it will turn your heart to stand as boastfulness and take in your hands for revenge.

Angriness, bitterness and resentment are the fruits of your works and actions. You don't show love, mercy and compassion to the Spirit who is living in the body of your neighbours. Satan will continue to put confusions in our life and will lead us to walk rebelliously to God. Most people won't understand that pride will destroy your life into pain, crying and suffering. This is why the world is broken and living in pain, crying and suffering. The world that God has created for all which is being considered as our paradise to live while we journey in this world for our limited times because we are only travellers on this world was formed as a zone for zombies. Most people are in trouble because of their ego and pride. Even you tell the truth they cannot accept it to be humble and accept the truth they will still believe in lies because that will suit their pride. They are angry when you pin-point the truth and let them realise that they are wrong. When you encountered a person like this you will be put to the test and challenges, if you're not aware to yourself you will turn on your ego to fight and bring yourself like also like a fool if you did not control your anger. Because they are ignorant, not aware and they don't understand the lie of their actions will not bring them peace, joy and happiness. Their actions will be paid them in full to suffering, divisions, discriminations and more confusion not knowing where to find the antidote for their suffering but multiplying their sufferings to others. And in their mind, the only way that makes pleases them is putting their heart in revenge not to be agreeable to fix the dispute and ended it peacefully. Their ego or pride is in-charge of their behaviour no wonder they are acting like as a beast. God hates pride but many human beings are a trap and marked their heart by the heart of the beast. Pride governs people's heart to turn evil to one another rather than being more considerate and loving to one another.

The history of life from the ancient time of the sons of Adam and Eve are misled by the wrong and deceiving God. For this pretending and false God puts angriness and jealousy in the hearts and minds of Cain therefore Cain did not give mercy to his brother and he killed his brother Abel. This false

God multiplied the confusions until to the times of Moses. As you will know in the story of the life of Moses, he is not a genuine Egyptian people. He came from the family of the Jews. Moses killed an Egyptians but this false God chooses Moses to stand as his child. He gave to Moses the Ten Commandments but his purpose is to confuse all the souls to fight and will continue to kill and waste the souls. Killings on that time are enormous between the Egyptians and the Jews. And until now the world is still broken and not in peace. War is still raging in the hearts of many. Forgiveness is very far to reach and give it to every soul so that we may have gained peace, love and harmony towards one another. We are being messed up by the beliefs of God of Abraham and Moses until now this is the reason why humans are fighting for the beliefs that they gain from their ancestors. Even Christians do not purely have the heart of real followers of Jesus as a Christian. Even Christian religions are lack of knowledge that is why they are fighting for the title to be the best and better religion in this world. Religion in this world did not help us to walk in harmony with God. As we can see there are so many religions in this world but the world is still broken and not in peace to turn like as back as a paradise to live.

World War 1 and World War 2 had a great history of killings and destroying not only the lives of many but also our Mother Earth which should be our paradise to live. What was the cause of their fighting is more about of invading one country to be part of them. They were ruling to captures one country but then afterwards what was the cause and damage that they do will cause only to the ridiculous act of nothing. These people who love to gain the richness of the world were also gone and not existing anymore into this planet. And the memories that they left for everything that they fight for ended only for foolishness and hypocrisy. They think that their life is forever and they will not depart in this world. Because of the lack of knowledge they didn't realise that we have given only a limited time to journey in this world but what they do. They put their hearts walking rebelliously to God for aiming to have the power and richness of this world. Their hearts are being ruled by the power of Satan. They don't show love and mercy to the Spirit that is living within them and to their neighbours because of the richness of the world. Many souls are being tortured, broken and ruined to be waste because of ego and pride. Because of pride, the world is in the great storm of confusion. They are so many tragic situations going on to the world. Pride is very good of confusing the mind of humans and deceiving the heart of all humanity to act like as a beast without considering that this place is also given to anyone who is travelling in this world. Discriminations, divisions and criticism are placed in everywhere because the pride which is the mark of the beast is fully alive in the hearts of many. Conscience is being shut down to their heart which is this conscience is the gift from God to us so that we may live in the presence of the Lord our Almighty Father. Most people reject their conscience and ignite their pride to ruin their souls and the souls of many. They have thought that their lives in this world have not to come to an end because they are all lack of knowledge about the true personality of God and they don't know God by heart for this reason they are acting evil to others. They didn't realise and recognise that we are all human beings walking, moving and living by Spirit and not by flesh alone. For a body without the spirit is dead and has no purpose for each own body is only from dust and this will return to dust.

Education in this world has no knowledge and wisdom to end the suffering in every hearts, families, society and county of the whole world. Education instead is one of the richness that belongs to this world and will accumulate problems in society. It is so ashamed that most people who had to finish their university and has degree are lack of knowledge towards integrity, humility and being considerate to others to go hand and hand towards into morality because they put in their mind that they are ahead to anyone especially to those who did not finish any degree. They make divisions, criticism and discrimination in the society. And for some who had finished their education have merited the rewards with a degree they are making competitions and comparisons to each and one another. Even they have a degree they don't have reach yet to have the knowledge and wisdom to go hand in hand to love one another. They lost the light in their heart for the love of their titles in this world. Wisdom, knowledge and understanding are still poor for they didn't get to the point to go beyond on everything. It is true that common sense does not grow in every brain. Our brain is the garden of our thoughts which is mainly the common denominator access of every action that comes to reality. We either grow flowers for charity in love, mercy and compassion or grow weeds for the insanity of doing evil.

Colours, cultures and nationality are also part of the problems in this world. With this people are also acting like beast they put their heart to discriminate, making divisions and criticism to other human beings because of these titles that human beings have carried into themselves. In the ancient times even from the stories of the life of people in the Old Testament, this is really happening until in our present time and in the futures of generations, this will not be changed. Unless we believe in Jesus by heart and we found the gift of the Holy Spirit in our lives. We were able to create ourselves as a new person by the grace and love of the Holy Trinity. We will transform ourselves into a conviction to what makes please to our Spirit rather than to our flesh. For we will have the wisdom that we are only travellers in this world and the key for our eternal life after our death here on earth is found in by being more caring, loving and respective to our soul and to the souls of other human beings who are also travelling in this world. For we will understand that our flesh is from dust and this will go to return to dust because this belongs to the richness of this world and not to God. The souls are the genuine true image of God that is living within us that is why we live and move our being and this is our lifeblood from God that we should need to care of, while we live and journeying in this world.

Religions are also part of the problems that will lead the heart and mind of human beings into confusion. As we can see there are so many religions in this world. And it is so sad that the world is still broken. No peace, no love, no unity and harmony in the hearts of human beings. Discrimination, division and criticism are also formed to cause havoc in every human being because of their religions. They were fighting for their religions for the title to be the best and chosen religions in this world. And yet no religions in this world can transform you as faithful to God like us Jesus. Without accepting Jesus in our heart, mind and soul and born again. We are not going to re-birth ourselves as a new person like as having the mind and the desire of the heart of Jesus to love God. Jesus is the way, the truth and life that will help us and enlighten our heart, mind and soul to be connected again in the hearts and minds of God. Our soul will be free from death by knowing the wisdom of the teachings and words of Jesus by heart. They will walk hand and hand by being loving and caring to the Spirit that is living into their body. They will resurrect their body out from the transgressions of sins by repentance and re-establish it again as the temple of the Lord. For our body is the temple of the Lord and we should keep it Holy by doing only what makes pleases to the Spirit rather than to our flesh. This is the reason why it is said that God is always with us when we take good care to our soul and the souls of our neighbours in this world.

Education, colours, cultures, nationality and religions are attached to all human being and through these titles that we are carrying humans are being blind not to love one another. We haven't had to gain the knowledge and understanding to lean on God for we are all boastful because of pride. Feed your conscience and you will love God who has given your life. Feed your pride and you will love Satan to destroy the lives of many into the condemnation of confusion of pain, crying, and suffering.

Money is the greatest source of evilness in this world. This is the reason why Jesus said we cannot serve two masters. We cannot love God and money at the same time. Because we will either love the one and hate the other. Honestly, money is evil and it is the main problems in every sovereign in all the families, society, and every county of the world. Many people love money because they think that money is the real source of life but not. Money was created only by humans but how about our Spirit? Is it created by the knowledge and wisdom by humans? Of course not, it is formed by the power and supernatural Spirit which whom we cannot see. Most people rely on money in their lives. And they think if they have the richness of money they may have power and they can do everything. But honestly, if you don't know God, who He is, you were able to deceive by the darkness of Satan to walk in his armies of being evil to your co-travellers in this world. Your mind has given you favour to what always pleases to your flesh. With money, adultery is easy for you to make lust and use your body into sexual immorality. Satan will give this to you. And if you are in a relationship with someone and you will be caught of being a cheater. Your relationship must have to an end because of your insanity about lust has broken the heart of a person who was you committed at. Trust and honesty are being ripped off because of your works some people will take you in revenge for your cheating them. Hatred and violence are on fire on your heart and to the one, you cheated at. Because of your money, it is easy for you to find more people to have relationships with you. And you will have to continue doing this sinful deed because you are not aware of yourself. After all, you are being used and manipulated by money and things. Your soul will be a trap on pain, crying and sufferings. Your fame because of your money will lead your soul to the destruction that will also lead to death on your soul once you were gone and has departed to this world. Cheating or adultery is one of the unforgivable sins and it is written in the law of the Ten Commandments. This is the reason why Jesus is calling to repent and sin no more against the Holy Spirit. Remember your body and the body of your neighbours who is your co-travellers in this world is the temple of God and the Holy Spirit and this must be kept Holy and out of sexual immorality. Repentance and change of heart can only be done while we still journeying in this world and not after our death in this world for this must be too late. Once our soul has departed to our body we human beings don't have the power to go back into our body anymore. Humans must learn to walk and live by truth of the Holy Spirit while they journey in this bold world which is maligned by Satan's darkness.

Another thing of sexual immorality is formed by people who cannot accept the truth of how they made by God. These people will pretend to be someone in who is not really in the gender that God made them. LGBT or GLBT is an initialising that stands for lesbian, gay, bisexual and transgender. These people are also journeying against the Holy Spirit because they use their body for sexual immorality. They cannot accept the truth and they choose aside what makes please to their flesh and now in this generation, many are being accepted to the society. And now even the church are doing blasphemy to the Holy Spirit by allowing these people to journey informed of same-sex marriage for not being righteous and obedient to God. They think it is really acceptable to God by creating more storms of confusion in society. Because we have been given the free will to live they think he/she can live as they like in this world without respecting the Spirit that is living in their bodies. They haven't thought about to care their soul this is the reason why at the end this will nail them into sufferings by condemning. It said that at the very end after our death in this world our soul will be put to judge according to our deeds and how did we believe in Jesus by heart. The problem in this world if you will follow your wisdom from God to walk and living by truth and Spirit, most people who are walking by what makes pleases their flesh will turn against you. But Jesus in His time in earth has thought about the people who were blessed by our Almighty Father. He said, "Blessed are the pure in heart, for they will see God. Blessed are the peacemakers, for they will be called children of God. Blessed are those who are persecuted because of righteousness, for theirs is the kingdom of heaven. Blessed are you when people insult you, persecute you and falsely say all kinds of evil against you because of me. Rejoice and be glad, because great your reward in heaven, for in the same way they persecuted the prophets who were before you. You are the salt of the earth. But if the salt loses its saltiness, how can it be made salty again? It is no longer good for anything, except to be thrown out and trampled underfoot. You are the light of the world. A town built on a hill cannot be hidden. Neither do people light a lamp and put it under a bowl. Instead, they put it on its stand, and it gives light to everyone in the house. In the same way, let your light shine before others, that they may see your deeds and glorify your Father in heaven. Do not think that I have come to abolish the LAW or the Prophets; I have not come to abolish them but to fulfil them. LGBT or GLBT are not able to create a formed and foundation as a real family. And the Spirit of God will not be multiplied with pure and real genuine love. Two men or two women who are both walking for sexual immorality will be in great troubles at their age. Jesus warns us to be on guard and does not be deceived by the false prophets. He said, for false messiahs and false prophets will appear and perform great signs and wonders to deceive, if possible, even the elect. Do not follow the crowd who is corrupt and will favour for injustices for this is not good in the eyes of the Lord. We should up hand ourselves to the righteousness that will set our souls free from any transgressions. Always remember that we are only travellers in this world and our flesh has come from the earth and this will return to earth. Make your soul as your priority to be careful of, while you still journeying in this world and God will bless you with an abundance of peace, love, hope, happiness, contentment that makes you feel complete. In every day of your life, you will be connected by the presence of the Lord. You will journey yourself with courage, confidence and wisdom not to worry or be afraid for you know deep in your heart God is the source of everything and He controls everything. He is the Alpha and Omega the beginning and an end. As long as God remains in your body you will be called still in purpose to manifest your life to be the light and salt for many. The Armageddon of God will be established in this world through you. You will stand with the courage to put the discernment of the heart of the unrighteous to bow in God and put their mind, heart and soul to repentance. The presence of the Holy Trinity in your life will guide you to move forward fearlessly. Your strength must come from the Spirit of the Almighty Father and you will fight always your battles on your knees. God will protect you from any harm. For God is your forever stronghold and endless strength in every moment of your life. Blessed are you for you will be called in this purpose for your heart, mind, and soul is secured in the presence and love of the Lord."

Before the Second Coming of Jesus
Matthew 24:6-15

And you will hear of wars and threats of wars, but don't panic. Yes, these things must take place, but the end won't follow immediately. Nations will go to war against nations and kingdoms against kingdoms. There will be famines and earthquakes in many parts of the world. But all this is only first of the birth pains, with more to come. Then you will be arrested, persecuted and killed. You will be hated all over the world because you are my followers. And many will turn away from me and betray and hate each other. And many of you who kill their brothers will become fugitives. And anyone will kill Cain will suffer vengeance seven times over. From that time until in the present time the mark of the beast is in charge to govern the world to put the souls of many in pain, crying and suffering. The pride which is the fruit of evil from the tree of knowledge between good and evil is easily getting angry or upset and if you did not balance yourself to have self-control your anger will turn to grudges, bitterness, angriness, resentment, hatred, violence, jealousy, complain, blame, evil and so on. The tactics of Satan is to ruin the souls of children of God and make them turn away from God by performing evilness in their hearts. The fruit of the Holy Spirit is completely opposite which is love, joy, peace, forbearance (patience), kindness, goodness, faithfulness, gentleness and self-control. This is the fruit we will have when we receive Jesus to live in our hearts. The fruits of the Holy Spirit will lead us to be more tender, caring, compassionate and merciful to the Spirit that is living in our bodies and to the bodies of our neighbours who are also our brothers and sisters. The Holy Spirit will help us to think before we act. Self-control is regulating our hearts not to be angry easily but be more prudent in morality, humility and integrity. The person who is working under the power of Satan is the person will be lost and will act like as an evil to his brother and sister in this world. Every human is a child of God by Spirit and not flesh. The flesh works for Satan, therefore, when the heart is full of lust and your body is being used for sexual immorality you are following Satan's desire to put your soul in transgression. This is the reason why most people end their lives in pain, crying and suffering. When you walk instead of by truth and Spirit you don't have the desire to love the riches of this world. You are not being manipulated by under in earthly desire. Your passion is to love and accept what do you have, God will give you the satisfaction to enjoy yourself for being who you are. Your desire is purely divine with love and charity. You don't put your heart to rely your life on food to feed your flesh. But you have a greater understanding that your body moves and lives because of the Spirit that is living inside of it. Satan will flee from you because your heart is purely working in the sight of the Lord. Now, this talent that God has given to you should need to multiply to others so that others will find also peace and harmony to be connected again in the present with our Almighty Father. We will put our hearts to work for peace to come at hand again this world as a paradise that God has created and prepared for each of His child that will travel in this world. Raptures will be understood by letting go of your pride and keeping your conscience alive in your mind, heart and soul. For you know deep in your heart that no one is the best or better than anyone else for the truth is no one man lives in this world eternally. The world will be reborn again as purely out of sins. For in the core of the heart of Mother Earth is human. Every human Spirit is important to God. Satan knows about it for he knows that the child of God has come from the same image of the evolution of Spirit which is the very source of life. The only way for Satan to hurt God is by seeing people fighting with each other. By multiplying and creating more violence, hatred and killings of the soul by committing sins and blasphemy towards the Spirit. This will favour to Satan and he is happy for his descendants are in demand as many like as the stars on the sky. And this is the one promise that this false God has given to Abraham. If you know the story of the life of Abraham with her wife Sarah, their works are full of blasphemy towards God and their neighbours which is our co-travellers in this world. For our real home is not here and not form by earth but in heaven where all the Spirit is living by intuition. We cannot hear it or see it by our sight but our heart is open to it if our senses and intuition are fully connected to the Holy Spirit. From then we were able to differentiate such things for God will give us the wisdom to understand everything that is behind on the stories or situation that we are standing at. Common sense will we call it for other Spirit will be connected to other Spirit. As we can see there are so many dialects in this world but God has given us to understand to interpret the words by the meanings of it. Common sense I found doesn't grow in every human's mind because they are blind to the truth they will keep on believing in lies even when you explain the truth clearly. Some people won't accept the truth because of their pride. They cannot accept that they are wrong. This is the reason why it is very difficult to correct an adult when their hearts are full of pride. They will reject you because they don't like to be corrected. For this kind of person, they think you ruined their dignity when you corrected them. Their mind was formed like a crab mentality this is the reason why the world is in great violence and war. For the love for their faces and their titles in this world it is better for them that their soul will be trapped in pain, crying and sufferings rather than to be at peace and free. Sins are the works of the fruit of Satan and the wages of this for your soul is dead. Some people who are being put to the test of this kind of people also find pain, suffering and heartaches and if you are not aware of yourself you turned like as these people. This is the reason why God sent His only begotten son Jesus to this world as our guiding light that will put our conscience to work with the Holy Spirit and encouraging our heart that we should need to have faith to believe and love God with all our mind, heart and soul with all our strength. Putting our heart to have hope and trust to God to be patience and silence during the storms of confusion in our life. When we put ourselves into silence by prayers and meditations God will boost us to know our ways to the way that we should go. He will journey with us and strengthen us to grow our Spiritual life and then after the storm, we are formed as a new person stronger than before. Our soul will sour like an eagle and we are more focus on journeying with the truth and Spirit. We are not formed to please anymore our flesh in earthly desires but we will protect our body as a sacred temple for God for He lives in there. And our intuition will tell us that God is always with us but to know him we should seek him by our hearts, not by our sight. This is the reason why it is said to look upon on the thing you cannot see for this is eternal, for the things that you will see from your sight is temporary. When we get to tap to the point to know this we will see the world in different ways not like before. As you wake everyday up you will be thankful for God has given you another day to do your purpose to love Him by being more considerate to the souls of many. You will have always the smile in your face to smile to others. And when some people don't smile at you in return you will be very understanding. You will think that he/she is not happy inside in your mind you might think there is something bothering in their mind. Their soul is not at peace because their heart might be in trouble of something. You were able to love and forgive your enemies also when you learn to walk and live by Spirit. People who will hurt you by ruining your dignity without justice by stabbing your back and gossiping your life with criticism and wrong judgement to others have the soul in sickness by allowing their pride to turns against you and being rebellious to God. These people are not happy in the inside and their actions towards you will let you know it. They don't show love and respect to the Spirit that is living within them therefore it is impossible for them to love your soul because even them they cannot love themselves. To love your neighbours as yourself has a deeper knowledge of understanding. It is not easily understood by human understanding. This is the reason why God said my thoughts are not your thoughts. We should need to be baptised and born again by the grace of the Holy Spirit. "Walking and living led by the grace of Holy Spirit we will be more to look after the Spirit of God that is living in the body of our neighbours." Therefore, if we did not put ourselves into repentance and seeking for the forgiveness of God, we will not be able to resurrect our souls by the power of darkness of Satan and Satan will not flee from us because the Holy Spirit is not alive in our hearts and body. We don't have the thought of God and Jesus. This is the reason why God said when we received the gift of His son Jesus we received God. Jesus is alive in this world by the presence of intuition. Therefore waiting for Jesus in this world will not come back to see Him from your sight but by revealing it into your heart. Jesus hearts and mind will rebirth into your life. This is the reason through repentance and receiving the gift of Jesus is the coming of Jesus for your life to save your soul. Yes, we will die in this world for we live here only temporary but our soul will be blessed by the grace and love of Jesus to journey in this world togetherness by the Holy Trinity. Once we depart in this world our soul will be secured by our good deeds by believing in Jesus. Our soul is welcome to come back in the kingdom of the Lord our Almighty Father. It is said that when before the coming of Jesus the world will suffer in wars, earthquakes and famines. The moon will turn red and there are more disasters but God has told us not to be fear for all these things will come to past then rapture. In Christian eschatology, the rapture refers to the predicted end-time event when all Christian believers—living and resurrected dead—will rise into the sky and join Christ for eternity. Rapture is about there are two personalities that one will leave and one will stay. It is not about two persons but it is about only one person with two characters inside in his/her body. The fruit that Adam and Eve that is eaten are formed our body as a tree of knowledge between good and evil. This is the reason why humans have these two characteristics of behaviour. We have the good and bad in the inside of our body. When we are born again by the Holy Spirit through repentance the wisdom of Jesus has been rebirth within us. Therefore we are not under any more by the power of Satan. The pride which is the mark of the beast that is living within us will leave and our soul will be resurrected by our conscience to stay. We conquer the grave for our soul will be free from sins and not to sins anymore for we know deep in our hearts once we come back to sin again our soul will be dead again. The love of God will never separate from us again. Our soul will journey by the presence of the Lord and we will create to rebirth our Mother earth with more plants and trees. More birds are chirping again in the sky. Rivers, streams and ponds will turn back again in life with more lovely fish. Butterflies, dragonflies, bees and any helpful insects will also come back as to life because of the plant and trees that we planted.

More animals will find more shelters to live and also their numbers will be multiplied again. Mining, illegal loggings and most smoke that comes to give pollutions in the earth will stop by automatically. Cigarettes, drugs and anything which is harmful to the body and the air will eliminate also for giving a fresh look in everywhere. Humans were understood that this is the cause of all climate change around the world. Humans will not love the richness of the world anymore for they know that they will depart from this world and this richness in this world cannot save our souls to live in paradise. We will journey as long as God is giving us our times to live on this planet. Our richness must be kept in our hearts by doing good to love the Spirit. Our Spirit will be reincarnation again to live in this world once we depart from our first journey. And our body will return to dust again for this will come from.

That is why I have my will to my family that once my Spirit leave my body, I will donate my organs to others who wanted to continue to live still on this planet. And the rest will be cremated and used it as fertilizers to the tree that gives fruit so that memories will last and be remembered into my family in that way. I don't need to spend money by putting my body on the ground without having a purpose. I'd like that make it useful for anyone and to the Mother Earth. When I told that to my Mum she did not agree with me. She says you know that every year there is all souls day and all saints day. She was asking me where they will go to see my tomb. I said if you see that my organs live in and remain to someone' s life part of me is in there still existing in this world but I told you that the best part of my body that is formed as dust after cremation will be put as fertilizers in the tree that bloom and give fruits. You can go to that tree and visit that tree and when you see it you will remember me that my dust has been buried in there as fertilizer. My Mum still not convinced in my idea but I said I don't want to take some earth to the Mother earth just for my tomb. I love that my body to makes has a purpose that's all. My body belongs to Mother earth and this I would like to should return as ashes. The legacy of my faith will be remembered in your hearts by all the good deeds that I made while I still exist on the earth by being connected to your Spirit. My love will never depart from you for we both keep this in our mind, heart and soul.

Writing this book is a way for me to give thanks and express my gratitude to God, and a way for me to show love for my neighbours. I would like to help all of humanity to find their ways to see God and His kingdom by living and journeying with the love by the Spirit and presence of the Lord in every day of our lives. My goal is to bring back the peace to the world and harmony that people will live without sins in their hearts so that when I am gone from this world because my life is only temporary like yours as well. It reminds me that I did something good for my other fellowmen. To renew their mind what makes pleases to God and walking obediently to God is by enlightening also their hearts to walk in life by truth and the grace of the Holy Trinity which is one triune God.

Corruption Is the Terror Attack of Confusion

The Pearl of the East on the sea which sighted be seen in the land of the Philippines is now going through a war on drugs. After Ferdinand Marcos lost his presidency the land of the Philippines has been accumulated to live in lies, which destroyed the country. Cory Aquino twisted the minds of the people for his love of power to ruin the dignity of the Marcos family with the help of betrayal with these two men. Marcos still wins the presidency, but because of betrayal of these two men who are working with him during his regime.

Juan Ponce Enrile Sr. (born February 14, 1924) is a Filipino politician and lawyer. He was a protégé of President Ferdinand Marcos, and served as Justice Secretary and then Defence Minister under the Marcos regime. He later became one of the leaders (along with General Fidel V. Ramos) of the 1986 People Power Revolution that drove Marcos from power and into exile. Enrile has continued to be a prominent politician since then; he was Senate President from November 8 until his resignation on June 5, 2013.

Fidel Valdez Ramos AFP PLH GCMG (Spanish: born Fidel Ramos y Valdez; March 18, 1928), popularly known as FVR and Eddie, is a retired Filipino general and politician who served as the 12th President of the Philippines from 1992 to 1998. During his six years in office, Ramos was widely credited and admired by many for revitalising and renewing international confidence in the Philippine economy. Before he was elected President, Ramos served in the Cabinet of President Corazon Aquino, first as chief-of-staff of the Armed forces of the Philippines (AFP), and later on, as Secretary of National Defence from 1986 to 1991. He was the father of the Philippine Army's Special Forces and the Philippine Police Special Action Force. During the historic 1986 EDSA People Power Revolution, Ramos was hailed as a hero by many Filipinos for his decision to break away from the administration of President Ferdinand Marcos and pledge allegiance and loyalty to the newly established government of President Cory Aquino. There should be huge allegations in the mind of these two men and intentionally hidden agenda for this works that Enrile and FVR have done. They used and manipulated Cory Aquino's mind for their intentions to prosper in their lives and to establish what is in their minds without caring for the people of the Philippines. "Enrile and FVR had a great part of the impact of confusion and catastrophe that multiplied in the land of the Philippines for being corrupt from three decades until now."

FVR and Enrile managed to twist and corrupt the mind of Cory Aquino to blame the family of Marcos for all the problems that were going on in the Philippines and for the assassination of her husband. FVR and Enrile are playing safely in silence for the cause of the tragedy, confusion and catastrophe that they made in the Philippines by accusing Ferdinand Marcos as a dictator. Aquino and Marcos are in the rage of the fight towards one another and people were 'confused' by also to fight each other without recognising the evil works of these two men. FVR and Enrile have clearly understood that they are insecure and jealous of Ferdinand E. Marcos, that is why even Marcos win in 1986 as President they lead to be a leader on EDSA People Power Revolution to drove Marcos from power into exile. These two evil men because of the love of power betrayed the family of Marcos and manipulated the families of Aquino to turn evil like them.

Corruption is an act of terrorism. It is so sad that these two evil men FVR and Enrile betrayed the whole country of the Filipinos. Ferdinand Marcos and Benigno Aquino are both friends but with these two men, FVR and Enrile manage to irrupt to end the ties of these two friends and families as enemies to one another. FVR and Enrile are both corrupt for grabbing the power. During Marcos' regime, the Philippines was known as the Tiger of Asia, and he made the lives of the Filipinos simple and prosperous. These two evil men (FVR and Enrile) must be accused of the damage that they have done to the Land of the Philippines for the past three decades because they are both corrupt and have twisted the minds of the Filipinos. They were injustices to blame Marcos for Martial Law but there is the truth about that Marcos did not proclaim the Martial Law alone. Marcos did ask the legislators to pass the law proclaiming the Martial Law because there is anarchy in the country. It is so sad that these two evil men, who betrayed Marcos, also betrayed the country and their fellowmen, making it dull for three decades for grabbing the power and destroying the country. Now in this present administration, President Rodrigo Duterte has restored the hope in most Filipinos' hearts to bring about change. Most Filipinos are tired and sick of the people who govern the country and lead it to poverty by grabbing the power to create chaos and anxiety not only in society but also in the lives of most families.

Drug abuse is rampant in the whole country because of the freedom in the Philippines. Most drug syndicates work to multiply their reach because their protectors work in the highest position of the government. Aquino Administrations allow these drug traffickers to boil in the country and turn the country to evaporate the life of many innocent souls. They drain the minds of people through drugs. They have lost their conscience to care for the lives of the families by not being loyal, loving, and caring to the members of their families for the sake of love of money and lust. Families are in great danger, trust is been ripped off because when one of their members in the family is high on drugs they forgot themselves and it is happening that innocent little child was been raped by the person who supposed to be that will protect them.

Children are turning rebellious and ending up on drugs. They will kill their parents when they are high on drugs. Because of poverty in the country, many have started to go out of the country just to earn money and help families back home. OFW *balikbayan* boxes are also touched by the crocodiles on the government. "OFW message to BOC (Bureau of Customs) No to opening balikbayan boxes." *Laglag-bala* [drop bullet] or *tanim bala* [plant bullet] in the airport have put troubles in the heart of many OFW and foreigners. President Aquino is not doing anything to stop these allegations in the airport.

Typhoon Haiyan, known as Super Typhoon Yolanda in the Philippines, was one of the most intense tropical cyclones on record, which devastated portions of Southeast Asia, particularly in the Philippines, on November 8, 2013. It is the deadliest Philippine typhoon on record, killing at least 6, 300 people in that country alone. Haiyan is also the strongest storm recorded on landfall. In January 2014, bodies were still being found. The cyclone caused catastrophic destruction in the Visayas, particularly on Samar and Leyte. According to UN officials, about 11 million people have been affected—many have been left homeless. The Aquino Government did not make any efforts to care for his fellowmen. Countries from all over the world came to the Philippines to help the Filipinos and donate money to support and fund the building of houses for the families that is been hit by Typhoon Haiyan. Tatay Digong who is known as Mayor Rodrigo Duterte of Davao took great effort to come to the disaster area to help and rescue people. Some foreigners and fellowmen from the country saw his love and care for his fellowmen and the land of the Philippines. People are asking about the money that was donated from all over the world, as it cannot be traced. The Aquino government has been accused of corruption. Filipinos are hungry for change and they saw Mayor Rodrigo Duterte as the only hope in the land, and as their only chance to change the country for good. Mayor Duterte saw that the greatest problem among the families and in the society is the consumption of drugs. On May 27, 2016, Mayor Rodrigo Duterte officially won the Philippines presidency. Controversial mayor, known as the Punisher, gets more than 16 million votes after campaign pledge to kill criminals. Duterte will officially assume the presidency on June 30, when Aquino's six-year term ends [EPA]. The constitution bars a president from running for two consecutive terms. During his campaign, Duterte, also known as The Punisher, vowed to kill suspected drug dealers and other criminals if elected president. Power of the people; how Rodrigo Duterte became the next president of the Philippines. After the historic 1986 EDSA People Power Revolution, Ramos, who betrayed

Ferdinand Marcos, was hailed as a hero by many Filipinos for his decision to break away from the administration of President Ferdinand Marcos and pledged allegiance and loyalty to the newly established government of President Aquino. Under Ramos, the Philippines experienced a period of political stability and rapid economic growth and expansion, as a result of his policies and programs designed to foster national reconciliation and unity. Ramos was able to secure major peace agreements with Muslim separatists, communist insurgents and military levels, which renewed investor confidence in the Philippine economy. Ramos also aggressively pushed for the deregulation of the nation's major industries and the privatisation of bad government assets. As a result of his hands-on approach to the economy, the Philippines were dubbed by various organisations internationally as Asia's Next Economic Tiger. During the tenure of Ferdinand Marcos, the Philippines was known as the Tiger of Asia. Now it revealed that all allegations that were happening in the Philippines from the past three decades were founded by FVR [Fidel Valdez Ramos] for secretly jealous to Ferdinand Marcos. FVR stole the presidency of Ferdinand Marcos for his own interest and to become popular after Cory Aquino's term of Presidency. FVR is the greatest corrupt officials secondly with his colleague Enrile who betrayed Marcos and put Marcos dignity into shame as a dictator in the country. FVR and Enrile are real manipulators and dictators who led Cory Aquino's mind corruption. FVR is a great pretender who lies. He betrayed the whole country by switching the mind of many innocent Filipinos to fight with each other. FVR tactics are really implemented to put the rage in the heart of many Filipinos and enjoying himself in silence for all this condemnation that is happening in the Philippines. Duterte is being questioned about extra-judicial killings [EJK] by human rights groups, and the news of all these killings are being spread as gossip all over the world. The VP Leni Robredo is turning against Duterte and blaming Duterte for the number of killings. This hypocrite woman who did not think first before accusing Duterte that the main factors of this killings are the protectors of drug trafficking is the same old Administration who has the eyes about drug traffickers. They are the ones who let in the drug traffickers and they were betraying one person by not going to be one with them in their groups. They are the one who can set up everything to kill their dealers when they can hint that this person is refusing to be not one with them anymore, and has in mind that before these people who turned against in their groups will be killed before it turns as an asset for the new Administration of Duterte. The corrupt are very good of doing corrupt strategies of blaming the cause of the problems even they are the main sources of problems of EJK for they are the drugs protectors. Their tactics of being corrupt are inherited by Fidel Valdez Ramos for he is the first corrupt political government who betrayed Ferdinand Marcos for grabbing the power just for self-interest. In NAGAleaks, FVR is the protector of Leni Robredo and Jessi Robredo in their drug business. Leni Robredo has been proven that she and her husband work under this corrupt man, Fidel Valdes Ramos. When Former late President Ferdinand E. Marcos burial his body at [libingan ng mga bayani]. FVR blast his angriness to the AFP and PNP and criticised the policy of new Administration Duterte. Most Filipino's believe that Leni Robredo's victory in her vice presidency is being cheated and corrupted by previous Administration Aquino. FVR is a person who is not happy to win another Marcos in politics. "This is probably the reason why Leni Robredo who works with him, won and stand to be proclaimed as vice president of the Philippines," If all Filipinos look back again to the past from when all the problems and confusion began they will find that all problems are enraged and Cory Aquino cannot manage to win her presidency in 1986 without the help of these two men which is Enrile and FVR who betrayed Marcos to put Marcos out to exile on the presidency. Cory Aquino is only used by these insecure men to Marcos as a puppet so that their desire must come easily and smoothly by deceiving the hearts and souls of many. Yes, Duterte is chosen by God to re-establish not only the country but also to help people to believe in God with a pure conscience to considerate the souls of his fellowmen with great power of love towards to humility and integrity. He knows that his life is only temporary and one day he will die but he wants to die with dignity and by staying faithful to God also to care all the souls of his fellowmen as the lambs of God.

Each innocent soul is important to God and this is the reason why Jesus was hated, criticised and persecuted in his time and was nailed to the cross. His purpose was to save the soul of the entire humankind and to help them have a great conscience and purity of heart. This is the reason why the opposition of Duterte is not happy, for Duterte wants to end the corruption in the government and to eliminate the drugs that drain the minds of many and turn them into zombies in the society. For their business of corruption and wanting to kill the innocent souls will come to an end. The horror that they put in the hearts of many will be abolished. All the criminals will be faced with their punishment. And most people who are afraid to die will be sent to rehab so that they find a new purpose of life to live and change their ways.

1 Timothy 6:4-5

Anyone who teaches something different is arrogant and lacks understanding. Such a person has an unhealthy desire to quibble over the meaning of words. This stirs up arguments ending in jealousy, division, slander and evil suspicions. These people always cause trouble. Their minds are corrupt, and they have turned backs on the truth. To them, a show of godliness is just a way to become wealthy.

Bible Tells About Corruption

We are living in a corrupt world which will only become more corrupt. Christ came to set us free from sin. We must repent and trust in the Blood of Christ. Believers are not to be conformed to this corrupt world. But we are to model our lives after Christ. We are seeing more and more of this world infiltrating Christianity, which is causing non-believers to slander the true believers.

Scriptures clearly warn us that we will see corrupt churches, pastors and many false converts. It is only going to get worse from here on so we must expose evil and spread the truth.

Deceitful people of this evil world are coming into our churches, spreading lies and false teachings about Christianity. We should never let corruption, which is schemed by Satan, cause us to lose focus on Christ. We are not to let them cause us to make excuses. Even though corruption is all around us, let's walk by the Spirit and continue to grow in Christ.

Galatians 6:8

Because the person who sows to his own flesh will reap corruption from the flesh, but the one who sows to the Spirit will reap eternal life from the Spirit.

2 Timothy 3:1–5

You must realise, however, that in the last days difficult times will come. People will be lovers of themselves, lovers of money, boastful, arrogant, abusive, and not obedient to their parents, ungrateful, unholy, unfeeling, uncooperative, slanderous, degenerate, brutal, and full of hatred towards what is good. They will become traitors, reckless, conceited, and lovers of pleasure rather than lovers of God. They will hold on to an outward form of godliness but deny its power. Stay away from this kind of people.

Believing in Jesus that He is the way, the truth and the light of the world will help us to see the kingdom of the Lord. No one can come to the Father Almighty God without the rebirth of our Spirit and developing wisdom and a heart like Jesus. We, human beings, will remain dull and dumb because of our actions and if we continue to deny ourselves to live faithfully in truth, and if we put ourselves in lies that please our ego and pride. Releasing the pride in our heart and accepting the truth will give us comfort not to worry in times of trouble but be more focussed towards ourselves to keep journeying in truth. We should give it to God to deal with this every confusion by prayers; sometimes the result will come more easily and favour you without stressing yourself. The proud and the boastful will ruin themselves with their egos at the right time.

Hidden Answer to the Confusion

Every adversity in our life was made and generated by every decision that we made and put in our hearts. To find the answer and the truth we should need to put back and analyse ourselves where the decision was made and where it all began. It is a calling for ourselves to look back on such things. Why we encountered this kind of confusion in our lives? What was wrong with the decisions that we made? Or if there is something we have to know if our decisions make us grow or gives us troubles. We need to re-channel our minds to see things in common and develop the sense to find the answer or solutions in better way.

Every solution can be found by reflecting on the past. By digging and finding the truth justice can be found through truthfulness and righteousness, and with actions driven towards to morality, humility and integrity.

Satan is not only a liar but also a deceiver who is very good in corrupting the minds and the hearts of people.

Terrorism springs from the mind of the corrupt. Their hearts are evil and rebellious to God. Satan is the greatest corrupt who will deceive and mislead the hearts of many to be unrighteous not only to God but also to their neighbours. This is the reason many souls are lost and broken to pieces. The world is ruled by the tactics of Satan and many go that way. Most people who are working under the power of Satan are also corrupt and turning against their neighbours and growing rebellious to God. They are like Zombies who like to kill the Spirit by destroying one another, want everybody to live in hatred, and in wicked and crooked ways. They are not honest to themselves for they know deep in their hearts what is kept inside. Liars are vipers and their works are not hidden from God, for God looks upon the heart and knows the purpose of your actions. He knows if your heart is pure and divine or evil to Him and His children. Jesus said that the body is the temple of the Lord, therefore, no action or motive of our actions is hidden from God. This is the reason why God said, "My thought is not your thoughts. No one man is higher than God."

Living in a Godly life, we must know the personality of God through Jesus Christ. Jesus is the one who will help us to awaken ourselves to take the journey with the power of the Holy Spirit. Great lessons in life are formed through experience, for it is a test that our faith will be tested by the fire of storms in life.

Jesus stays the same yesterday, today and tomorrow, for His love and wisdom endures forever. Jesus' Spirit is fully alive in this world. He did not depart, for his teachings and love guide us that we may able to have access to see God and His kingdom when we learn to seek on God whole-heartedly. God's plan for all of his children is to teach ourselves to walk and live by truth and Spirit. For his kingdom is revealed in the nature of Spirit and not in the richness of this world. Our soul is eternally bound to the power of The Holy Spirit. Jesus' teaching is noble and divine and I consider that true religion is established and it is the covenant of the Lord is found in the heart of Jesus. No religion in this world can ever save your soul and to know God by heart but only by Jesus.

Jesus is the light of the world, and to be called the Child of God we must submit our hearts to believe in Jesus and have the heart like Jesus. We will walk our days in the presence of the Holy Trinity till the end that our times end to life on this planet. Sacred memories live forever in the heart of people who have been touched, also their souls to walk and live by the grace of Spirit.

God is Spirit.

God is love.

God is eternal and His power endures forever.

1 Peter 1:7

These trials will show that your faith is genuine. It is being tested as fire tests and purifies gold, though, your faith is far more precious than mere gold. So when your faith remains strong through many trials, it will bring you more praise and glory and honour on the day when Jesus Christ is revealed to the whole world.

Facts That Prove Jesus Christ Is God

- ✓ Jesus was conceived by the Spirit of God.
- ✓ Jesus is the firstborn child of the Holy Spirit.
- ✓ Jesus' soul is the offspring of the Holy Spirit.
- ✓ From the beginning of the creation of the world, Jesus is with the Father. He is one of the endeavours of Spirit that Almighty Father is talking to. On the sixth day of creation, God is saying to all endeavour of Spirit saying.

We will create man both male and female with our image and likeness. This is the reason why both male and female are equally having the same Spirit from God. The soul that has been bestowed to humans is the Spirit and is from God. The soul is our life that comes from heaven. And at the end of our time here on earth, our soul will return to Spirit and will face judgement according to our deeds while we are in the earth. And our flesh will return to dust because it is dust and that was from the earth. This is the reason why Jesus said to the Jews, "Truly, truly, I say to you, before Abraham was, I am."

- ✓ Jesus was formed from the Spirit like God before God created heaven and earth. He is Spirit and He is God. This is the reason that Jesus said that He and the Father are one. Because they are both equally Spirit.
- ✓ By heart, Jesus knows that His genealogy did not come from the flesh of Abraham but the Spirit of the Holy Spirit. Jesus knows that God is Spirit and worshippers of God must worship God in the Spirit.

This is the kind of worshippers that our Almighty Father seeks.

✓ Jesus warned people that there are sins, which are forgivable but not those that make us commit blasphemy or slander the Holy Spirit.

✓ If you will have the heart like Jesus, you will understand by heart that Jesus was proclaiming the name of the Holy Spirit as the Highest God, which is the Father and God of His soul, and each soul.

✓ The soul of Jesus is the Lamb of God and this is the same image that comes from the Blood of God. By his stripes, your soul will be purified and cleansed to be enlightened and resurrected from death.

✓ Jesus said, "Do not worry who has the power to kill your body but don't have the power to kill your soul. Sin is death and the wage of sins is death for our soul." This is the reason why Jesus said, "Repent and sin no more."

✓ Jesus said, "When you believe in me, you believe in the Father who sent me. Always remember that the Holy Spirit is God, for He is Spirit and not human." The Holy Spirit is the God and Father of Jesus' soul and every human soul. But when you turn against the Holy Spirit your soul will not be recognised as the Child of God, and you will not remain the brother/sister of Jesus Christ. Always remember that each body is the temple of the Holy Spirit and the Holy Spirit dwells among us. The Holy Spirit is the owner of our soul and flesh. The Holy Spirit is also the Spirit of truth. He knows everything about us, therefore, we cannot hide the truth from the Holy Spirit. He knows the fruits of our hearts. Therefore, Honour the Holy Spirit as the Father and God of your soul or else when you turn against the Holy Spirit. Your soul will be cast out from heaven and condemned to eternal fires of hell.

Luke 17:20-21

Once, on being asked by the Pharisees when the kingdom of God would come, Jesus replied, "The coming of the kingdom of God is not something that can be observed, nor will people say, 'Here it is,' or 'There it is,' because the kingdom of God is in your midst."

Keeping our body sacred and as a Holy temple of the Holy Spirit and home for our soul will lead our heart to see heaven here on earth. The kingdom of God will be added unto us. Our soul will be free from death to inherit eternal life. But if we try to destroy the house of God for sexual immorality and for lustful desires that belong to the world, our body will be transformed into purgatory for our souls.

1 Corinthians 3:16-17

Don't you know that you yourselves are God's temple and that God's Spirit dwells in your midst? If anyone destroys God's temple, God will destroy that person; for God's temple is sacred, and you are that temple.

The body is sacred and this is the temporary house of our soul while we travel the world. Therefore, we must keep our body sacred and only use for Spiritual purposes and not for lustful desires. Therefore, if the Holy Spirit is still giving the life to your soul and body to travel in this world, you must repent and seek for pardon in the Holy Spirit while the Holy Spirit is still with you to be called.

We must accept that we are not just human beings but deeply we are so-called Spiritual beings that live by the grace of Love from one eternal God. We must accept in our hearts that we human beings are not living alone and not living only by food or by the power of money but by the grace and power of the Holy Spirit.

✓ Jesus is the Messiah, No one soul can see and no one soul can enter the kingdom of God unless we have been baptised and born again as the Holy Spirit through the grace of the blood (soul) of Jesus Christ.

✓ Jesus is the way of truth and life. No one can come to the Father except through the name of Jesus Christ.

If all heart, mind and soul in every nation will be renewed to be baptised and born again in the Holy Spirit, the world will be filled by the presence of the Holy Spirit. God will eliminate sickness and death, and unite all mankind to stand as one eternal family in the Spirit. No soul will be lost and will die anymore for death has been defeated by the power of the Holy Spirit. Many hearts will change and repent, the souls of the people who are still alive in this world will be resurrected from death. And this will be the day of rapture.

God will establish a perfect government here on the world for all His children and make the earth renewed as a paradise again.